PRAYING WITH
CELTIC CHRISTIANS

PRAYING WITH
Celtic
Christians

George McLean

This edition first published in 1996
Triangle
SPCK
Holy Trinity Church
Marylebone Road
London NW1 4DU

First published by Triangle in 1988 with the title
*Praying with Highland Christians: A Selection from
Poems of the Western Highlanders* by G. R. D. McLean.

British Library Cataloguing-in-Publication Data
A catalogue record of this book is available from
the British Library

ISBN 0-281-04978-5

Typeset by Rowland Phototypesetting Ltd,
Bury St Edmunds, Suffolk
Printed in Great Britain by
BPC Paperbacks Limited.

Contents

Contents

GREAT GOD
OF ALL GODS

The Creed Prayer

O great God of all gods, I believe
That thou art the Father eternal of all life above;
O great God of all gods, I believe
That thou art the Father eternal of goodness and love.

O great God of all gods, I believe
That thou art the Father eternal of each holy one;
O great God of all gods, I believe
That thou art the Father eternal of each lowly one.

O great God of all gods, I believe
That thou art the Father eternal of each clan of men;
O great God of all gods, I believe
That thou art the Father eternal of earth of our ken.

Chief and God of the hosts, I believe
That thou art the creator and maker of heav'n on high,
That thou art the creator and maker of soaring sky,
That thou art the creator of oceans that under lie.

Chief and God of the hosts, I believe
That thou art the creator and warper of my soul's thread,
Thou my body's creator from dust and earth-ashes' bed,
Thou my body's breath-giver and thou my soul's domain
    bred.

O Father, bless to me my members,
O Father, bless my soul and being,
O Father, bless to me life's embers,
O Father, bless belief and seeing.

Father eternal, Chief of hosts, I believe
That my soul thou with thine own Spirit of healing didst
   mend,
And thou thy belov'd Son in covenant for me didst send,
And thou the blest blood of thy Son for my soul didst
   expend.
      Father eternal, Chief of all, I believe
That thou at baptising the Spirit of grace didst extend.

      Father eternal, Chief of mankind,
      Enwrap my body and soul entwined,
      Safeguard me tonight in thy love shrined,
      The saints' aid tonight my shelter kind.

      For thou has brought me up from the night
      Unto this morning's most gracious light,
      Great joy unto my soul to provide,
      And excelling good to do beside.

      O Jesu Christ, all thanks be to thee
      For the many gifts bestowed on me,
      For each sea and land, each day, each night,
      For each mild, each fresh, each weather bright.

I am giving thee worship with my whole life every hour,
    I am giving thee assent with my whole power,
With my fill of tongue's utterance I am giving thee praise,
    I am giving thee honour with my whole lays.

I am giving thee reverence with my whole knowledge
upcaught,
 I am giving thee offering with my whole thought,
I am giving extolling with my whole good intent's flood,
 I am giving thee meekness in the Lamb's blood.

I am giving thee loving with my devotion's whole art,
 I am giving kneeling with my whole desire,
I am giving thee liking with my whole beating of heart,
 I am giving affection with my sense-fire;
I am giving mine existing with my mind and its whole,
 O God of all gods, I am giving my soul.

  My thought, my deed, my word, and my will,
  My mind, my brain, my state and my way,
  I beseech thee to keep me from ill,
  To keep from hurt and from harm today;
  To keep me from grieving and from plight,
  In thy love's nearness to keep this night.

  O may God shield me, and may God fill,
  O may God watch me, and may God hold;
  O may God bring me where peace is still,
  To the King's land, eternity's fold.

  Praise to the Father, praise to the Son,
  Praise to the Spirit, the Three in One.

Christmas Carol

Ho to the King! blessed is he!
Ho to the King! blessed is he!
Ho to the King of whom we sing!
    Ho! ro! joy let there be!

This night is the eve of greatest birth,
    Born is the Son of Mary Maid,
The soles of his feet have touched the earth,
    Son of glory above displayed,
    Heaven and earth to him aglow
        As he comes below,
        Ho! ro! joy let there be!

Heavenly joy and peace upon earth,
    Behold his feet have reached the place;
O worship the King, hail the Lamb's birth,
    King of the virtues, Lamb of grace,
    Ocean and earth to him alit
        As he doeth it,
        Ho! ro! joy let there be!

The gleam of distance, the gleam of sand,
    Roar of waves with a tide that sings
To tell us that Christ is born at hand,
    Saving Son of the King of kings,
    Sun on the mountains high ashine
        Reveals him divine,
        Ho! ro! joy let there be!

The earth and the spheres together shine,
    The Lord God opes the starry floor;
Haste, Son of Mary, assistance mine,
    Thou Christ of hope, and joy's wide Door,
        On hills and ranges, golden Sun,
            Behold, it is done!
            Ho! ro! joy let there be!

The Star-Kindler

The Kindler of the starry fires
Behold, cloud-pillowed like desires,
And all the aery feathered quires
         Are lauding him.

With heavenly music down he came
Forth from the Father of his Name,
While harp and lyre in song acclaim
         Applauding him.

O Christ, thou refuge of my love,
Why lift not I thy fame above?
When saints and angels full enough
         Are songing thee.

O sweet MacMary of all grace,
How glist'ring white thy pure fair face,
How rich the joyful pasture place
         Belonging thee!

O Christ my loved beyond the flood,
O Christ, thou of the Holy Blood,
By day and night outswell my bud
         Of praising thee.

The Voice of Thunder

O God of the elemental might,
O God of the mysterious height,
O God of the stars and cloudsprings bright,
   O King of kings to bestow!
   O King of kings to bestow!

Thy joy the joy of the raindrops' play,
Thy light the light of the lightning's spray,
Thy war the war of the heavenly fray,
   Thy peace the peace of the bow,
   Thy peace the peace of the bow.

Thy pain the pain of groaning and clash,
Thy love the love of the sudden flash,
That lasts for aye like the music's crash,
   Till the end of ends below,
   Till the end of ends below.

Thou pourest thy grace, refreshing shower,
Upon men in grief and duress hour,
Upon men in straits and danger's power,
   Without cease or stint to show,
   Without cease or stint to show.

Thou Son of Mary of Paschal feat,
Thou Son of Mary of death's defeat,
Thou Son of Mary of grace replete,
   Who wast and art, shalt be so
   With the ebb and with the flow;
      Who wast and art, shalt be so,
      With the ebb and with the flow!

Sunrise

The eye of God, the God who is great,
The eye of the God of glory's state,
The eye of the King of hosts that strive,
The eye of the King of all alive,
Pour out as time and moments go,
Pour out on us thy gen'rous flow,
   On us thy gentle gen'rous flow.

Thou sun of joy, glory to thee,
To thee be glory, O thou sun,
Face of the God of life to see,
Face of the morning rising one,
   To thee be glory, O thou sun.

Jesus-Praise

It were as easy, Lord, for thee
As to wither the sapling new
Anew to green the withered tree
Were it thy will the thing to do,
    O Jesu, Jesu, Jesu,
    Unto whom all praise is due.

There is no plant in all the land
But blooms replete with thy virtue,
Each form in all the sweeping strand
With joy replete thou dost endue,
    O Jesu, Jesu, Jesu,
    Unto whom all praise is due.

All life that is within the sea,
In river every dwelling thing,
All in the firmament that be
Thy goodness overflowing sing,
    O Jesu, Jesu, Jesu,
    Unto whom all praise is due.

Each single star fixed in the sky,
Each bird arising on the wing,
They that beneath the sun do lie
Thy goodness all proclaiming sing,
    O Jesu, Jesu, Jesu,
    Unto whom all praise is due.

Doxology

As it was, as it is, and as it shall be
Evermore, God of grace, God in Trinity!
With the ebb, with the flow, ever it is so,
God of grace, O Trinity, with the ebb and flow.

THIS DAY

Prayer this Day

My prayer to thee, O God, pray I this day,
Voice I this day in thy mouth's voicing way,
As hold the men of heaven this day I hold,
Spend I this day as spends thine own household,
Under thy laws, O God, this day I go,
As saints in heaven pass pass I this day so.

Thou loving Christ who hangedst on the tree,
Each day, each night, thy compact mindeth me;
Lie down or rise unto thy cross I cede,
In life and death thou health and peace indeed.

Each day thy mercies' source let me recall,
Gentle, gen'rous bestowing on me all;
Each day in love to thee more full be I
For love to me that thou didst amplify.

From thee it came, each thing I have received,
From love it comes, each thing my hope conceived,
Thy bounty gives each thing that gives me zest,
Of thy disposing each thing I request.

God holy, loving Father, of the word
Everlasting, this living prayer be heard:
Understanding lighten, my will enfire,
Begin my doing and my love inspire,
My weakness strengthen, enfold my desire.

Cleanse heart, faith confirm, sanctify my soul,
Circle my body, and my mind keep whole;
As from my mouth my prayer upriseth clear,
May I feel in my heart that thou art here.

And, O God of life, do thou grant to me
That thou at my breast, at my back shalt be,
That thou give my needs as befits the gold,
The above-world crown to us promise-told.

And, Father beloved, grant thou that to me,
From whom each thing that is outfloweth free,
No tie too strict, no tie too dear between
Myself and this beneath-world here be seen.

O my God, in thee all my hope I set,
Father of the heav'ns, my living hope yet,
My great hope with thyself that I may be
In the far world that cometh finally.

Father, Son, Spirit, Holy Trinity,
Three in One Person and the One in Three,
Infinite and perfect, world without end,
Changeless through endless life, let praise ascend.

From the Darkness

O gentle Christ, ever thanks to thee,
That thou from the dark hast raised me free
And from the coldness of last night's space
To the gentle light of this day's grace.

O God of all creatures, praise to thee,
As to each life thou hast poured on me,
My wish, my word, my sense, my man praise,
My thought, my deed, my fame, and my ways.

The Lighthouse Prayer

O God, who from last night's sweet rest dost me convey
To the light of joy of the day that is today,
From the new light of this day be thou bringing me,
Unto the light of guidance of eternity,
    From the new light today be thou bringing me
    Unto the guiding light of eternity.

Rising Prayer

Thou King of the moon and of the sun,
Of the stars thou lov'd and fragrant King,
Thou thyself knowest our needs each one,
O merciful God of everything.

Each day that our moving steps we take,
Each hour of awakening, when we know
The dark distress and sorrow we make
To the King of hosts who loved us so;

Be with us through the time of each day,
Be with us through the time of each night,
Be with us ever each night and day,
Be with us ever each day and night.

Morning Thanksgiving

That I have ris'n today, O God, the thanks be unto thee,
        To the rising of this life itself again;
O God of every gift, to thine own glory may it be,
        To the glory of my soul likewise a gain.

O great God, unto my soul give thine aid and make it full
        With the great aiding of thine own mercy whole;
Even as I am covering all my body with the wool,
        With the shadow of thy wing cover my soul.

God, be helping mine avoiding every sin that life fills,
        And my forsaking the cause of sinful ways;
And as flees the mist of morning on the crest of the hills,
        May there clear off from my soul each evil haze.

The Pilgrim's Hope

I bathe my face in water fresh,
As the sun his nine rays doth spread,
As Mary washed her Son's fair flesh
In the generous milk white-shed.

May mercy be my lips' attire,
May kindness to my face be lent,
May chasteness be on my desire,
And wisdom be in mine intent.

Love Ma.y laid her one Son on
May all the world give unto me;
Love Jesus-giv'n to Baptist John
Grant I give to each one I see.

Son of God, be at the outset,
Son of God, be surety, friend;
Son of God, make straight my way yet,
Son of God at my seeking's end.

The Morning Dedication

     Let thanks, O God, be unto thee,
From yesterday who broughtest me
The morning of today to see,
Joy everlasting to earn whole
With good intention for my soul.
For every gift of peace to me,
Thoughts, words, deeds, and desires from thee
Each one bestowed, I dedicate.
And I beseech, I supplicate
That thou may'st keep me from offence,
Tonight my aiding and defence,
For the sake of thy wounding red,
With thine offering of grace outspread.
     Let thanks, O God, be unto thee.

Morning Prayer

O Jesus Christ, all thanks be to thee,
Who hast brought me safely through last night,
To the morning joy of this day's light,
To win everlasting life for me,
Through the blood that thou didst shed for me.

O God, for ever praise be to thee,
For the blessings thou bestow'st on me –
For my food, my work, my health, my speech,
For all the good gifts bestowed on each,
O God, for ever praise be to thee.

I pray thee now to shield me from woe,
From sinning, this night to consecrate,
God of the poor, and I poor and low,
O Christ of the wounds, thy wisdom great
Along with thy grace on me bestow.

May the Holy One make claim on me,
And protect me on the land and sea,
Step by step leading me on my way
To the City of e'erlasting day,
Peace of the City that lasts for aye.

Each Day and Night

Each day in justice let me speak,
Each day thy chastening marks, O God, display,
Each day in wisdom let me speak,
Each night at peace with thee, at peace each day;

Each day thy mercy's causes store,
Each day may I compose to thee a song,
Each day give heedance to thy law,
Each day string out, O God, thy praises strong;

Each day love let me give to thee,
Each night, O Jesu, grant I do the same,
Each day and night laud give to thee
Or dark or light, for goodness of thy Name,
Or dark or light,
Each day and night.

Somerled's Supplication

O Being of life! O Being of peace!
O Being of time, and time without cease!
O Being, infinite eternity!
O Being, infinite eternity!

In good means of life be thou keeping me,
In all good intending, o keeping be,
Be keeping me always in good estate,
Far better than I know to supplicate,
    O better than I know to supplicate!

Be shepherding me for all this day long,
Relieve my distress, relieve me from wrong,
Enfold me this night with thine arms' embrace,
And pour upon me thy bountiful grace,
    O pour upon me thy bountiful grace!

My speaking and words do thou guard for me,
And strengthen for me my love, charity,
Illumine for me the stream I must o'er,
And succour thou me when I pass death's door,
    O succour thou me when I pass death's door!

Life-Consecration

Jesu MacMary, have mercy upon us;
Jesu MacMary, thy peace be upon us;
  Where we shall longest be,
  With us and for us be,
  Amen, eternally.

Jesu MacMary, at dawn-tide, the flowing,
Jesu MacMary, at ebb-tide, the going;
  When our first breath awakes,
  Life's day when darkness takes,
Merciful God of all, mercy bestowing,
  With us and for us be,
  Merciful Deity,
  Amen, eternally.

Condition and lot, to thee make them holy,
Condition and lot, to thee take them wholly,
  King of all kings that be,
  God of all things that be,
  Amen, eternally.

Our rights and our means, to thee make them holy,
Our rights and our means, to thee take them wholly,
  King of all kings that be,
  God of all things that be,
  Amen, eternally.

Our body and heart, to thee make them holy,
Our body and heart, to thee take them wholly,
  King of all kings that be,
  God of all things that be,
  Amen, eternally.

Each body and heart, the whole of each being,
Each day, each night also, thine overseeing,
   King of all kings that be,
   God of all things that be,
   Amen, eternally.

Thoughts

'Tis God's will I would do,
My own will I would rein;
Would give to God his due,
From my own due refrain;
God's path I would pursue,
My own path would disdain;

For Christ's death would I care,
My own death duly weighed;
Christ's pain my silent prayer,
My God-love warmer made;
'Tis Christ's cross I would bear,
My own cross off me laid;

Repentance I would make,
Repentance early choose;
Rein for my tongue would take,
Rein for my thoughts would use;

God's judgment would I mind,
My own judgment close-scanned;
Christ's freedom seizing bind,
My own freedom in hand;
Christ's love close-scanned would find,
My own love understand.

The New Year

God bless to me the new day that is here,
Nor ever yet before designed for me;
It is to bless thy countenance so dear
This time, O God, thou givest me to see.

O bless thou unto me my seeing eye,
And mine eye bless each one that it doth see;
My neighbour I will bless who liveth nigh,
My neighbour give his blessing unto me.

O God, give me a heart of cleanliness,
Nor be I from thy watching eye offstood;
And unto me my wife and children bless,
Bless unto me my stock and livelihood.

Prayer for the Day

Do thou, O God, bless unto me
   Each thing mine eye doth see;
Do thou, O God, bless unto me
   Each sound that comes to me;
Do thou, O God, bless unto me
   Each savour that I smell;
Do thou, O God, bless unto me
   Each taste in mouth doth dwell;
Each sound that goes unto my song,
   Each ray that guides my way,
Each thing that I pursue along,
   Each lure that tempts to stray,
The zeal that seeks my living soul,
The Three that seek my heart and whole,
   The zeal that seeks my living soul,
   The Three that seek my heart and whole.

THE PATH I WALK

A Journey Prayer

This day to me, God, do thou bless,
This very night, God, blessing give,
Thou God of grace, o do thou bless
All days and all the times I live;
  Thou God of grace, o do thou bless
  All days and all the times I live.

God, bless the path I walk above,
God, bless the earth beneath my toes;
God, bless me, give to me thy love,
O God of gods, bless rest, repose;
  God, bless me, give to me thy love,
  O God of gods, bless my repose.

The Travel-Shield of God

Almighty Lord, thou God of might,
   Shield me this night and sustain,
Almighty Lord, thou God of might,
   This night and each eve again.

Sain me and save me from mischief whole,
   And from sin save me and sain,
Sain me my body and my soul,
   Each dark and each light again.

Bless me the land my hope doth prize,
   Bless me the thing faith shall see,
Bless me the thing my love descries,
   God of life, bless what I be.

Bless the journey whereon I go,
   And bless the ground under me,
Bless the matter I seek to know,
   Glory-King, bless what I be.

East or West

May the everlasting Father throw
      His shield to shade you
Every east and west that you may go,
      His shield to aid you.

Fear by Night

God before me, God behind,
God above me, God below;
On the path of God I wind,
God upon my track doth go.

Who is there upon the shore?
Who is there upon the wave?
Who is there on sea-swell roar?
Who is there by door-post stave?
Who along with us doth stand?
God and Lord on either hand.

I am here abroad, without,
I am here in want, in need,
I am here in pain, in doubt,
I am here in straits indeed,
I am here alone, afraid,
O God, grant to me thine aid.

The Roadmaker

God be shielding thee by each dropping sheer,
God make every pass an opening appear,
God make to thee each road a highway clear,
   And may he take thee in the clasp
       Of his own two hands' grasp.

By Upland and Brae

On every steep to thee God's shielding shade,
On every climb to thee may Christ give aid,
On every rise the Spirit's filling made,
Thy way by upland or by plainland braeed.

The Pilgrim's Aiding

May God be with thee in every pass,
Jesus be with thee on every knoll,
Spirit be with thee by water's roll,
   On headland, on ridge, and on grass;

Each sea and land, each moor and each mead,
Each eve's lying-down, each rising's morn,
In the wave-trough, or on foam-crest borne,
   Each step which thy journey doth lead.

Sea Blessing

God the Father almighty, whose kindness cheers,
O Jesu the Son of the sorrows and tears,
O thine aiding aid, Holy Spirit, endears!

The Three-One e'er living, great, lasting, o'erhead,
Who across the Red Sea the Israelites led,
And Jonah to land from the sea-monster sped,

Who led Paul with his company setting sail,
Forth from the sea-stress, from the wave-torment's flail,
From the storm that was great, from foul-weather gale,

When the tempest poured on the Lake Galilee,
The disciples cried out in their misery,
And thou Jesu of sleeping didst still the sea.

O sain us, set us free, and sanctify best,
On our helm, O King of the elements, rest,
And steer us in peace to our voyage's quest.

Gentle winds, kindly, pleasant, fragrant to waft,
Not an eddy, nor swirl, nor whirl for our craft,
But safe let her ride and unscathed fore and aft.

All things of thy bounty, O God, we beseech,
For thy will so and word accordingly teach.

Ship Consecration

HELMSMAN	Be the ship blest.
CREW	By God the Father blest.
HELMSMAN	Be the ship blest.
CREW	And by God the Son blest.
HELMSMAN	Be the ship blest.
CREW	By God the Spirit blest.
ALL	God the Father,
	And God the Son,
	God the Spirit,
	Blessing give blest,
	Be the ship blest.
HELMSMAN	What can afear
	With God the Father near?
CREW	Naught can afear.
HELMSMAN	What can afear
	And God the Son is near?
CREW	Naught can afear.
HELMSMAN	What can afear
	And God the Spirit near?
CREW	Naught can afear.
ALL	God the Father
	And God the Son,
	God the Spirit,
	Be with us here
	And ever near.

HELMSMAN	What care is bred,
	Being of all o'erhead?
CREW	No care is bred.
HELMSMAN	What care is bred,
	The King of all o'erhead?
CREW	No care is bred.
HELMSMAN	What care is bred,
	Spirit of all o'erhead?
CREW	No care is bred.
ALL	Being of all,
	The King of all,
	Spirit of all,
	Over our head
	Eternal fall,
	Near to us sure
	For evermore.

The Helmsman

God of the elements, glory to thee
For the lantern-guide of the ocean wide;
On my rudder's helm may thine own hand be,
And thy love abaft on the heaving sea.

A Sailor's Prayer

Thou Being who Jonah didst safely land
Out from the bag of the sow of the sea,
Bring thou myself to the beckoning strand
With lading and ship entrusted to me.

GIVE US, O GOD . . .

The Gates of the Kingdom

Give us, O God, the needs the body feels,
  Give us, God, the need-things of the soul;
Give us, O God, the balm which body heals,
  Give us, God, the soul-balm which makes whole.

Bliss give us, O God, of repentance-ease,
  Bliss give us, God, of forgiveness sought,
Away from us wash thou corruption's lees,
  From us wipe the blush of unclean thought.

O great God, thou who art upon the throne,
  Give to us the heart repentance true,
Forgiveness give us of the sin we own –
  The sin inborn and the sin we do.

Give us, O God, a yearning that is strong,
  And the crown of glory of the King;
Give us the safe home, God, for which we long
  In thy kingdom's lovely gates to sing.

May Michael, archangel warrior white,
  Keep down hostile demons of the fall;
May Jesus Christ MacDavid guide our flight
  And give lodging in his peace-bright hall.

The Meal

Give us, O God, our morning bread,
The soul by body nourishéd;
Give us, O God, the perfect bread,
Sufficiently at evening fed.

Give us, O God, milk-honey yield,
The strength and cream of fragrant field;
God, give us rest, our eyelids sealed,
Thy Rock of covenant our shield.

Give us this night the living fare,
This night the saving drink be there;
This night, for heaven to prepare,
Give us the cup of Mary fair.

Be with us ever night and day,
In light and darkness, be our stay,
With us, abed or up, alway,
In talk, in walk and when we pray.

Grace before Food

Be with me, O God, at breaking of bread,
And be with me, O God, when I have fed;
Naught come to my body my soul to pain,
O naught able my contrite soul to stain.

Thanks after Food

O God, all thanks be unto thee,
O God, all praise be unto thee,
O God, worship be unto thee,
For all that thou hast given me.

As thou didst give my body life
To earn for me my drink and food,
So grant to me eternal life
To show forth all thy glory good.

Through all my life grant to me grace,
Life grant me at the hour of death;
God with me at my leaving breath,
God with me in deep currents' race.

O God, in the breath's parting sigh,
O, with my soul in currents deep,
Sounding the fords within thy keep,
Crossing the deep floods, God be nigh.

God of the Sea

O God of the heaving sea,
Give the wave fertility,
Weed for enriching the ground,
Our life-giving pouring sound.

Before Prayer

The Father who created me
With eye benign beholdeth me;
The Son who dearly purchased me
With eye divine enfoldeth me;
The Spirit who so altered me
With eye refining holdeth me;
In friendliness and love the Three
Behold me when I bend the knee.

O God, through thine Anointed One,
The fullness of our needs be done –
Grant us towards God the love ordained,
Grant us towards man the love unfeigned;
Grant us the smile of God's good face,
Grant us God's wisdom and God's grace;
Grant us to fear and reverence still,
Grant in the world to do thy will
As done in heaven by saintly hands
And myriad of angelic bands;
Each day and night, each dawn and fall,
Grant us in kindness, Lord of all,
Thy nature's tincture at our call.

For Forgiveness

On this day, on this thy night,
　　O God be with us, Amen.
On this thy day, on this thy night,
　　To us and with us, Amen.

It is full clear within our sight
That since we came to this world's light
We have deserved thy wrath's despite;
　　O God be with us, Amen.

O God of all, o thine own wrath,
Stretch, O God, thy forgiveness forth,
　　To us forgiveness, Amen,
　　Forgiveness with us, Amen,
　　To us and with us, Amen.

Thine own forgiveness to us give,
Merciful God, by whom we live,
Merciful God of all, forgive,
　　O God be with us, Amen,
　　To us and with us, Amen.

Anything that to us is ill,
Or that may stand against us till
We come where is our longest day,
　　Lighten it to us aright,
　　O darken its ugly light,
　　O banish it from our sight,
Forth from our heart chase it away,
For everlasting and for aye,
　　Ever and ever, Amen.
For everlasting and for aye,
　　Ever and ever, Amen,
　　O God be with us, Amen.

Confession

Jesu, give unto me the forgiveness of sin,
Jesu, be mine erring not forgotten within,
Jesu, give me the grace of repentance's school,
Jesu, give me the grace of forgiveness in full,
Jesu, give me the grace of submissiveness due,
Jesu, give me the grace of sincerity true,
Jesu, give me the grace of humility's part,
My confession to make at this time from my heart,
At throne of confession condemnation to own
Lest condemnation I find at the judgement throne;
Jesu, give me the strength and the courage, alone
At throne of confession condemnation to own
Lest condemnation I find at the judgement throne.
More easy is a season of chastening to me
Than a descent unto death for eternity.
Jesu, give unto me all my guilt to confess
With the urgency of death's importunateness.

> Jesu, take pity, o take pity on me,
> Jesu, upon me have mercy, mercy whole,
> Jesu, do thou take me, o take me to thee,
> Jesu, give thou aid, o give aid to my soul.

> Sin is of grief a cause, o a cause,
> And a cause of sore anguish is death,
> But repentance is of joy a cause
> And the cleansing stream's life-giving breath.

O Shepherd, who leavest the ninety and nine,
Good Shepherd, who seekest the sheep that hath slipt,
The angels of heav'n will have joy that is mine
That in the confession-stirred pool I am dipt.

O my soul, lift up and rejoicing be,
God willeth for thee an atonement above,
Seize his hand while it is stretched out unto thee
To announce to thee an atonement of love.

Withdraw not thy hand O my God, from me here,
O Chief of the chiefs, o withdraw not thy hand,
For Lord Jesus Christ's sake my Saviour so dear,
That I go not to death's everlasting land.

For Grace

I am bending low my knee
In the eye of those who see,
Father who my life supplied,
Saviour Son who for me died,
Spirit who hath purified,
In desire and love to thee.

Be the blessing heaven-sent
Richly poured on penitent;
City-Prince of firmament,
O forbear thy punishment.

Grant us, Glory-Saviour dear,
God's affection, love and fear,
God's will to do always here
As above in heaven clear
Saints and angels do not cease;
Day and night give us thy peace,
   Give each day and night thy peace.

The Pilgrim's Relief

Each one, O God, do thou relieve
In all his suffering on land or sea,
In grief, or wound, or in tears, receive,
To thy peaceful halls his leader be
        As day doth fade.

I am weary and weak and chill,
Weary of travelling on land and sea,
Of crossing moor and the foam-white hill,
Grant peace anigh of thine ease to me
        As day doth fade.

O my God's Father, lovéd one,
Let the care of my crying suffice;
With thee I would wish atonement done,
Through the witness and the ransom price
        Which thy Son paid;

With Jesus to find restfulness
In the blest habitation of peace,
In the paradise of gentleness,
In the fairy-bower of release
        Mercy-arrayed.

He who was Crucified

Thou who wert hanged upon the tree,
By people condemned, crucified there,
   Now that grown old and grey I be,
Pity, O God, my confession-prayer.

I wonder not my sins are great,
I am a clattering cymbal poor,
   I was profane in youth's estate,
Forlorn in my ageing at the door.

Those to whom God hath no desire
Are people who lie, people who swear;
   Fountain-tears, hot-springing as fire
Rather would he, and genuine prayer.

Death Prayer

O God, of thy wisdom do thou give,
O God, of thy mercy that I live,
Of thine abundance, O God, provide,
In face of each strait be thou my guide.

God, of thy holiness consecrate,
O God, of thine aiding aid my state,
Of thy surrounding, O God, invest,
And in my death's knot give of thy rest;
 O of thy surrounding to invest,
 And in my dying hour of thy rest!

Happy Death

Thou God of salvation great, outpour
On my soul thy graces from above
As up the sun of the heights doth soar
And on my body outpours its love.

Needs must that I die and go to rest,
Nor know I where or when it will be;
But if of thy graces unpossest
So I am lost everlastingly.

Death of anointing, repentance due,
Death of joy, death of peacefulness giv'n;
Death of grace, death of forgiveness true,
Death that endows life with Christ and heav'n.

Death's Ford

O may the Father clasp you in his hand,
His fragrant loving clasp bring you to land,
Across the flooding torrent when you go
And when the stream of death doth blackly flow.

GOD MY LIFE-WHOLE

God my Guide

O God with thy wisdom be my guide,
God with justice chastising provide,
O God with thy mercy be mine aid,
God my protection with might arrayed.

O God with thy fullness be my fill,
God with thy shadow cloak shield me still,
God with thy grace my fullness be done,
For the sake of thine Anointed Son.

Jesu the Christ of King David's line,
Visiting One of the Temple shrine,
Sacrifice Lamb of the Garden pure,
Whose death did my salvation procure.

Morning Protection

Be the eye of God between me and each eye,
Between me and each purpose God's purpose lie,
Be the hand of God between me and each hand,
Between me and each shield the shield of God stand,
God's desire between me and each desire be,
Be God's bridle between each bridle and me,
    And no man's mouth able to curse me I see.

Between me and each pain the pain of Christ show,
Between me and each love the love of Christ grow,
Between me and each dearness Christ's dearness stay,
Christ's kindness between me and each kindness aye,
Between me and each wish the wish of Christ found,
Between me and each will the will of Christ bound,
    And no venom can wound me, make me unsound.

Be the might of Christ between me and each might,
Be the right of Christ between me and each right,
Flow of the Spirit between me and each flow,
Between me and each lave the Spirit's lave go,
Between me and each bathe the Spirit's bathe clean,
    And to touch me no evil thing can be seen.

Rest Benediction

Bless to me, O God, the moon above my head,
Bless to me, O God, the earth on which I tread,
Bless to me, O God, my wife and children all,
Bless, O God, myself to whom their care doth fall;
   Bless to me my wife and children all,
Bless, O God, myself to whom their care doth fall.

Bless, O God, the thing on which mine eye doth rest,
Bless, O God, the thing to which my hope doth quest,
Bless, O God, my reason and what I desire,
Bless, thou God of life, o bless myself entire;
   Bless my reason and what I desire,
Bless, thou God of life, o bless myself entire.

Bless to me the partner of my love and bed,
Bless to me the handling of my hands outspread,
Bless to me, O God, my compass compassing,
Bless, o bless to me sleep-angel mine a-wing;
   Bless to me my compass compassing,
Bless, o bless to me sleep-angel mine a-wing.

The Soul's Healer

Healer thou of my soul,
At eventide keep whole,
Keep me at morning ray,
Keep me at full noonday,
As on my rough course I fare.

Safeguard me and assist
That this night I subsist,
I am tired and astray,
And so stumbling my way,
Shield thou from sin and from snare.

God's Aid

God to enfold,
God to surround,
God in speech-told,
God my thought-bound.

God when I sleep,
God when I wake,
God my watch-keep,
God my hope-sake.

God my life-whole,
God lips apart,
God in my soul,
God in my heart.

God Wine and Bread,
God in my death,
God my soul-thread,
God ever breath.

Before Me

Before me be thou a smooth way,
Above me be thou a star-guide,
Behind me o be thou keen-eyed,
For this day, this night, and for aye.

I weary and heavy am driv'n,
Lead me on to the angels' place;
'Twere time now I went for a space
To Christ's court and the peace of heav'n;

If only thou, God of life, give
Smooth peace for me, at my back near,
Be as star, as helmsman to steer,
From smooth rest till rising I live.

Jesus the Encompasser

Jesu! Only-begotten mine,
  God the Father's Lamb sacrificed,
  Thou didst give the body's blood-wine
  From the grave-death to buy me right.
My shield, my encircler, my Christ, my Christ!
For each day, each night, for each dark, each light.
  My shield, my encircler, my Christ, my Christ!
  For each day, each night, for each dark, each light.

Jesu! uphold me and be nigh,
  My triumph, treasure, thou art now.
  When I lie down, when stand, be by,
  Whenever I watch, when I sleep.
My aid, my encircler, MacMary thou!
My strength everlasting, MacDavid, keep;
  My aid, my encircler, MacMary thou!
  My strength everlasting, MacDavid keep.

The Holy Spirit

O Holy Ghost
Of pow'r the most,
Come down upon us and subdue;
From glory's place
In heaven space,
Thy light of brilliance shed as dew.

Lov'd Father One
To each bare son,
From whom all gifts and goodness flow,
Our hearts enshrine
With mercy's shine,
In mercy shield from harm and woe.

God, without thee
Naught can there be
Within man that can a price gain;
King of kings, lo!
Without thee so
Ne'er a sinless man without stain.

All on thee stayed,
Thou the best aid
Against the soul of wildest speech;
Food thou art sweet
O'er other meat;
Sustain and guide at all times each.

The stiff-joint knee,
O Healer, free,
'Neath thy wing warm heart's hardness lie;
The soul astray
Out of thy way,
O swing back his helm lest he die.

Each foul thing seen
Early make clean,
Each that is hard grace-soften through,
Each wound or blow
That pains us so,
Healer of healers, whole renew!

Thy people must
In thee place trust,
God, grant diligence to do it;
Help them each hour
With sev'nfold pow'r,
Thy gift, gen'rous Holy Spirit!

The Holy Ghost Distilling

May the Holy Ghost distilling,
   Down from heaven forth to ground,
Grant me aid and goodness filling,
   That my prayer be firmly bound
The King of life's great throne around.

May the Holy Ghost with blessing
   Wing the prayer I send as dove
In the fitting state and gracing
   Of thy holy will above,
O Lord my God of life and love.

Be I in God's love, God's dearness,
   Be I in God's will, God's sight,
Be I in God's choice, God's nearness,
   Be I in God's charge, God's might,
And be I in God's keep aright.

As thine angels fair, untiring,
   As thy saints, household entire,
They in heav'n above desiring,
   So on earth may I desire,
With Holy Ghost aflame in fire.

Chief of Chiefs

Chief of chiefs beyond my ken,
    O Chief of chiefs, Amen.

God be with me lying down,
    And God be with me rising,
In the sunlight flying down
    God with me, supervising,
No joy nor any light without him,
    Nor any light without him.

Christ be with me sleeping hours,
    And Christ be with me waking,
Through all watches aiding powers,
    Christ with me undertaking,
No day nor any night without him,
    Nor any night without him.

God be with me to protect,
    The Spirit there to strengthen,
Lord be with me to direct
    As span of life doth lengthen,
No time, no year, no hope, no fear,
No age, no space, no work, no place,
No depth nor any height without him,
    Nor any height without him.

Ever, evermore, Amen,
    O Chief of chiefs, Amen.

The Path of Right

With God be my walking this day,
With Christ be my walking this day,
With Spirit my walking this day,
The Threefold all-kindly my way;
Ho, ho, ho! the Threefold all-kindly I pray.

My shielding this day be from bane,
My shielding this night be from pain,
Ho, ho! soul and body, the twain,
By Father, Son, Spirit, amain;
By Father's, by Son's, and by Holy Ghost's sain.

The Father be he shielding me,
And be God the Son shielding me,
The Spirit be he shielding me,
As Three and as One let them be:
Ho, ho, ho! as Three and as One Trinity.

Afloat and Afield

I pray to God my petition and rite,
To Mary's Son, to the Spirit of right,
In distress to assist afloat, afield;
The Three to give succour, the Three to shield,
The Three to watch me by day and by night.

God and Jesus and the Spirit so pure,
Possess me, and shield me, assist me sure,
Order my path and before my soul go
In hollow, on ' ill, and on plain below,
Afloat, afield, the assisting Three sure.

God and Jesus, Holy Spirit of right,
Give shielding and saving to me in might,
As Three and as One, the great Trinity,
By my back, by my side, and by my knee,
As through the drear world-storm my steps alight.

The Three Everywhere

The Three who are over my head,
The Three who are under my tread,
The Three who are over me here,
The Three who are over me there,
The Three who are in the earth near,
The Three who are up in the air,
The Three who in heaven do dwell,
The Three in the great ocean swell,
    Pervading Three, o be with me.

The Three

In the Father's name,
And in the Son's name,
In the Spirit's name,
Three the same, One in name;

Father be my friend,
And Son be my friend,
Spirit be my friend,
Three to send and befriend.

God my holiness,
Christ my holiness,
Spirit holiness,
Three to bless, holiness.

Help of hope the Three,
Help of love the Three,
Help of sight the Three,
And my knee stumbling free,
From my knee stumbling free.

THIS NIGHTFALL

The Soul Petition

O Jesu, this nightfall,
Who dost fold-herd the poor,
Without sin thou at all
Who didst suffer full sore,
By the wicked's decree,
Crucified thou for me,

From ill be my safeguard,
And safeguard me from sin,
Save my body and ward,
Make me holy within,
O Jesu, this nightfall,
Nor leave me till light fall.

O endow me with might,
Virtue-Herdsman of light,
Do thou guide me aright,
Do thou guide me in might,
Thine, O Jesu, the might,
Keep me safe until light.

Nightfall

Come I this day to the Father of light,
Come I this day to the Son, morning bright,
Come I to the Holy Ghost great in might;
Come I this day with God, blessing to find,
Come I this day with Christ, promise to bind.
Come I with the Spirit of potion kind.

O God, and Spirit, and Jesu, the Three,
From the crown of my head, O Trinity,
To the soles of my feet mine offering be;
Come I with my name and my witnessing,
Come I with my contrite heart, confessing,
Come I unto thee, O Jesu my King –
O Jesu, do thou be my sheltering.

The Soul-Shrine

God, give thy blest angels charge to surround
   Watching over this steading tonight,
A sacred, strong, steadfast band be they found
   To keep this soul-shrine from mischief-spite.

Safeguard thou, O God, this household tonight,
   Themselves, their means of life, their repute,
Free them from danger, from death, mischief-spite,
   From jealousy's and from hatred's fruit.

O grant thou to us, O God of our peace,
   Whate'er be our loss a thankful heart,
To obey thy laws here below nor cease,
   To enjoy thee when yon we depart.

Night Blessing

The dwelling, O God, by thee be blest,
And each one who here this night doth rest;
My dear ones, O God, bless thou and keep
In every place where they are asleep;

In the evening that doth fall tonight,
And in every single evening-light;
In the daylight that doth make today,
And in every single daylight-ray.

Smooring the Fire

The holy Three
For saving be,
To act as guard,
To aid and ward
The hearthstone fire,
The house entire,
The household all
As eve doth fall,
And night enthrall,
This evening light,
And o this night!
Each evening light,
Each single night,
So may it be,
O holy Three,
Amen to me.

Resting Supplication

O God, preserve the house, the fire, the kine,
All those who here tonight in sleep recline.
Preserve myself, my love-fold children's band,
From attack keep us and from harm withstand;
Keep us this night from foes and hatred shun,
For the dear sake of Mary Mother's Son,
Here and each where tonight they resting dwell,
This evening's night and every night as well,
 This evening's night and every night as well.

Undressing Prayer

O thou great God, thy light grant to me,
O thou great God, thy grace may I see,
O thou great God, thy felicity,
And in thy health's well cleanse me pure-white.

O God, lift from me mine anguish sore,
O God, lift from me what I abhor,
O God, lift from me vanity's store,
And lighten my soul in thy love's light.

As I shed off my clothing at night,
Grant that I shed off my conflict-plight,
As vapours lift off the hill-crests white,
Lift thou my soul from the mist of death.

O Jesu Christ, O MacMary One,
O Jesu Christ, O thou Paschal Son,
My body shield in thy shield-cloak spun,
My soul made white in thy white grace-breath.

Bedside Prayer

O Jesu, the one who art sinless quite,
Thou humble King of the meek and the poor,
Who wast brought low and crucified so sore
By sentence of the evil men of spite,
Do thou defend and shield me for this night
From traitor-ways and Judas-dark-steal flight.

My soul on thine own arm, O Christ, to lie,
Thou art the King of the City of Heaven,
Thou it was, Jesu, who my soul didst buy,
For by thee was my life-sacrifice given.

Do thou protect me because of my woe,
For the sake of thy passion, wounds, thy blood,
Take me in safety tonight as I go
Climbing up near to the City of God.

Night Sanctification

Father, bless me and my body keep,
  Father, bless me in my soul;
Father, bless me through this night of sleep
  In my body and my soul.

Father, bless me as I live my days,
  Father, bless me in my creed;
Father, bless me in my binding ways
  To my life and to my creed.

Father, sanctify to me my speech,
  Father, sanctify my heart;
Father, sanctify my portion each
  In my speech and in my heart.

Resting Blessing

In name of Rabbi Jesus of avail,
And of the Spirit of the balm so blest,
In the name of the Father of Israel,
      I lay me down to rest.

If any trick or evil threat there be,
Or secret that on me fate doth contrive,
May God encompass me and make me free,
      Mine enemy forth drive.

In the name of the Father richly dear,
And of the Spirit of the balm so blest,
In name of Rabbi Jesus who is near,
      I lay me down to rest.

O God, encompass me and give me aid,
From this hour till my death the hour invade.

Repose

Of virtues thou Being,
> Shield me with thy might,
Thou Being decreeing
> And of the starlight.

This night be my compass,
> For body and soul,
This night be my compass,
> Each night compass whole.

Aright be my compass
> 'Twixt earth and the sky,
Law-tight be my compass
> And for my blind eye;

That eye-caught belonging
> And that unread here;
That clear to my longing
> And what is unclear.

The Trinity at Night

With God will I lie down this night,
And God will be lying with me;
With Christ will I lie down this night,
And Christ will be lying with me;
With Spirit I lie down this night,
The Spirit will lie down with me;
God and Christ and the Spirit, Three,
Be they all down-lying with me.

Lord it is night

The night is for stillness
Be still, in Gods presence

It is night after a long day
What has been done has been done;
What has not been done has not been done
    Let it be

The night is dark.
Let our fears g the darkness g our
own lives and g the world
        Rest in you.

The night is quiet.
Let the quietness g your peace enfold us
All dear to us, and those who have no peace

94

Sleep-Dedication Prayer

O my God and O my Chief,
In morning light to thee I pray,
    O my God and O my Chief,
Again this night to thee I pray.
    I give unto thee belief,
I give my mind, my yea and nay,
    I give unto thee my lief,
Body, and soul that lives for aye.

    Mayest thou be unto me
Chieftain and master for my sway,
    Mayest thou be unto me
Shepherd and guardian lest I stray,
    Mayest thou be unto me
Herdsman and guide that I obey,
    O Chief of chiefs, with me be,
God of the skies, Father for aye.

The night heralds the dawn
Let us look expectantly
To a new day
new joys
new possibilities
In your name we pray   Amen

Quietude of Sleep

O God of life, this night
O darken not to me thy light,
O God of life, this night
Close not thy gladness to my sight,
O God of life, this night
Thy door to me o shut not tight,
O God of life, this night
Refuse not mercy to my plight,
O God of life, this night
Quell unto me thy grieving slight,
O God of life, this night
Crown thou to me thy joy's delight,
O crown to me thy joy's delight,
O God of life, this night.

Come my Light
My Lord, my way
Come my Lantern
Night & day
Come my Healer
Make me whole
Come my Saviour
Protect my soul
Come my King
Enter my heart
Come Holy Presence
Never depart

Sleeping Prayer

My soul and my body this night I place
On thy sanctuary, O thou God of Grace,
On thy sanctuary, O Jesus Christ, here,
On thy sanctuary, Spirit true and clear,
    They who would stand to my cause, the Three,
          Nor coldly turn their backs on me.

Thou Father, righteous and kind one who art,
Thou Son, who o'er sin didst play victor's part,
Thou Holy Spirit of the mighty arm,
Give keeping to me this night from all harm;
    They who would my right uphold, the Three,
          This night and always keeping me.

The Cross of Christ

Christ's cross 'twixt me and the folk of the hill
   That stealthily out or in do go,
The cross of Christ betwixt me and each ill,
   Each evil will, each misliking woe.

Be the angels of heaven shielding me,
   The heavenly angels for this night,
Be the angels of heaven shielding me
   Soul and body together aright.

The circle of Christ my compass around,
   From every spectre, from every bane,
And from every shame that comes to confound
   In darkness, and in power to give pain.

The circle of Christ my compass in might,
   My shielding from every harmful thing,
My keeping from each destruction this night
   Approaching me on destroying wing.

GOD, BLESS

The Homestead

O God, bless my homestead,
  Bless thou all in there.
O God, bless my kindred,
  Bless thou my life-share.

O God, bless my speaking,
  Bless thou what I say,
O God, bless my seeking,
  Bless thou all my way.

O God, sin decreasing,
  Increase thou belief.
O God, woe surceasing,
  Ward off from me grief.

God, from guilt be my shield,
  With joy be I filled.

O God, of my body
  Let naught harm my soul
When to great MacMary
  I enter in whole
In fellowship union
  Of his communion.

Family Blessing

Bless, O our God, the fire here laid,
As thou didst bless the Virgin Maid;
O God, the hearth and peats be blest,
As thou didst bless thy day of rest.

Bless, O our God, the household folk
According as Lord Jesus spoke;
Bless, O our God, the family,
As offered it should be to thee.

Bless, O our God, the house entire,
Bless, O our God, the warmth and fire,
Bless, O our God, the hearth alway;
Be thou thyself our strength and stay.

Bless us, O God Life-Being, well,
Blessing, O Christ of loving, tell,
Blessing, O Holy Spirit spell
With each and every one to dwell,
  With each and every one to dwell.

House Blessing

God bless the house from ground to stay,
From beam to wall and all the way,
From head to post, from ridge to clay,
From balk to roof-tree let it lay,
From found to top and every day
God bless both fore and aft, I pray,
Nor from the house God's blessing stray,
   From top to toe the blessing go.

For the Household

God, bless the world and all that in it dwell,
God, bless my partner, children dear as well,
God, bless the eye that stands set in my head,
And, God, the handling of my hand o bless;
What time I rise in morning's earliness,
What time I lie down late upon my bed,
   My rising bless in morning's earliness,
   And my late lying down upon my bed.

God, guard the household members and the hall,
God, consecrate the mother's children all,
God, all the flocks and young in safety keep;
Be after them and tend them from the fold,
What time the herds ascend the hill and wold,
What time I lie me down in gentle sleep,
   When slow the herds ascend the hill and wold,
   When tired I lie me down in peace to sleep.

The Prayer of Baptism

The little wave for thy form complete,
The little wave for thy voice so meet,
The little wave for thy speech so sweet.

The little wave for thy means requite,
The little wave for thy generous plight,
The little wave for thine appetite.

The little wave for thy wealth at hand,
The little wave for thy life in land,
The little wave for thy health to stand.

Nine waves of grace to thee may there be,
Saving waves of the Healer to thee.

The fill of hand for thy form complete,
The fill of hand for thy voice so meet,
The fill of hand for thy speech so sweet.

The fill of hand for thy mouth so small,
The fill of hand for thy fingers all,
The fill of hand to make strong and tall.

The fill of hand for the Father one,
The fill of hand for God's only Son,
The fill of hand for the Spirit done.

Nine fills of hand for thy grace to be,
In name of the Three-One Trinity.

The Mother's Farewell

The blessing of God, be it thine,
The blessing of Christ, be it thine,
The blessing of Spirit be thine,
On thy children be it to shine,
On thee and thy children to shine.

The peace of God, may it be thine,
The peace of Christ, may it be thine,
The peace of the Spirit be thine,
Thy whole span of life to refine,
All thy days and life to refine.

Shield of God in the pass be thine,
Aid of Christ in the gorge be thine,
Spirit-water in stream be thine,
Every going thou dost design,
A land or an ocean design.

The Father eternal's shield thine,
Upon his own lit altar-shrine;
The Father's shield always be thine,
Eternal from his altar-shrine
Lit up by gold taperflame-shine.

Grace of Love

Thine be the grace of love when in flower,
  Thine be the grace of humble floor,
Thine be the grace of a castled tower,
  Thine be the grace of palace door,
  Thine be the pride of homeland place
          And its grace.

The God of life to encompass thee,
Loving Christ encompass lovingly,
The Holy Ghost encompasser be
Cherishing, aid, enfolding to send
          To defend.

The Three be about thy head to stand,
  And the Three be about thy breast,
The Three about thy body at hand
  For each day, for each night of rest,
  The Trinity compassing strong
          Thy life long.

Peace between Neighbours

Peace between neighbours near,
Peace between kindred here,
Peace between lovers dear,
In love of the King of us all.

Peace man with man abide,
Peace man to wife allied,
Mother and bairns to guide,
And peace of the Christ above all.

Bless, O Christ, bless my face,
My face bless every face,
Christ, bless mine eye with grace,
Mine eye give a blessing to all.

The Peace of Everlasting

Peace of all felicity,
Peace of shining clarity,
Peace of joys consolatory.

Peace of souls in surety,
Peace of heav'n's futurity,
Peace of virgins' purity.

Peace of the enchanted bowers,
Peace of calm reposing hours,
Peace of everlasting, ours.

The Encompassing of the Three

The compassing of God be upon thee,
    God of the living encompassing.

The compassing of Christ be upon thee,
    The Christ of loving encompassing.

The compassing of Spirit be on thee,
    Holy Ghost laving encompassing.

The compassing of the Three be on thee,
    Encompassing Three preserving thee,
    Encompassing Three preserving thee.

The Clasping of God

May the Father everlasting
Himself take you, round you casting
His own gen'rous arm engrasping,
His own gen'rous hand enclasping.

God's Grace Distilling

The grace of God on you distil,
The grace of Christ bedewing fill,
The grace of Spirit flowing still
Each day and night upon you pour
Of this life's share for you in store;
  O day and night upon you pour
  Of this life's share for you in store.

The Trinity Pouring

Yours be the blessing of God and the Lord,
The perfect Spirit his blessing afford,
The Trinity's blessing on you outpoured
With gentle and gen'rous shedding abroad,
So gently gen'rously for you unstored.

The Eye of the Great God

May the great God's eye, beholding
God of glory's eye be seeing,
Eye of Virgin's Son be freeing,
Gentle Spirit's eye, enfolding,
Shepherd's aiding to thee showing
    In every time, in every clime,
    Each hour on thee outpouring be
In a gentle, gen'rous flowing.

The Three Rich and Generous

The eye of God with thee to dwell,
The foot of Christ to guide thee well,
The Spirit's pouring shower to swell
Thy rich and gen'rous fountain-well.

Good Wish

Eye that is good be good to thee,
Good of liking unto thee be,
   The good of my heart's desire.

Sons that are good to thee be born,
Daughters good to thee fair as dawn,
   The good of my sense's fire.

Thine the good of the good wide sea,
Thine the good of land fruitfully,
   Good of Prince of heav'nly quire.

Christ's Safe-Guarding

O the Christ's guarding that it may
Safe shield you ever and a day.

A Joyous Life

A joyous life I pray for thee,
Honour, estate and good repute,
No sigh from thy breast heaving be,
From thine eye no tear of suit.

No hindrance on thy path to tread,
No shadow on thy face's shine,
Till in that mansion be thy bed,
In the arms of Christ benign.

God's Blessing be Thine

God's blessing be thine,
And well may it spring,
The blessing divine
In Thine every thing.

Deep peace of the Running Wave to you
Deep peace of the Flowing Air to you
Deep peace of the Quiet Earth to you
Deep peace of the Shining Stars to you
Deep peace of the Son of Peace to you

Peace for this Life

The peace of God be unto you,
The peace of Jesus unto you,
The peace of Spirit unto you,
Be peace unto your children too,
Peace unto you, your children too,
Each day and night let there be peace
Till of this world your portion cease.

The Creator's Love

God the Father uncreate
       Above,
Your Creator Potentate
       In love,
Be with you in lovingness
       And bless.

The Kindly Lantern

The very self of the Mary Virgin's Son
   To you a kindly lantern may he be,
   Over your head a guiding, shining one
For the wide rough ocean of eternity.

Joke
Book

Jeremy Strong once worked in a bakery, putting the jam into three thousand doughnuts every night. Now he puts the jam in stories instead, which he finds much more exciting. At the age of three, he fell out of a first-floor bedroom window and landed on his head. His mother says that this damaged him for the rest of his life and refuses to take any responsibility. He loves writing stories because he says it is 'the only time you alone have complete control and can make anything happen'. His ambition is to make you laugh (or at least snuffle). Jeremy Strong lives near Bath wit⸻   ⸻flying cow.

Are you feeling silly enough to read more?
THE BEAK SPEAKS
CHICKEN SCHOOL
DINOSAUR POX
GIANT JIM AND THE HURRICANE
I'M TELLING YOU, THEY'RE ALIENS!
THE INDOOR PIRATES
THE INDOOR PIRATES ON TREASURE ISLAND
KRANKENSTEIN'S CRAZY HOUSE OF HORROR
KRAZY KOW SAVES THE WORLD – WELL, ALMOST
LET'S DO THE PHARAOH!
PANDEMONIUM AT SCHOOL
PIRATE PANDEMONIUM
THE SHOCKING ADVENTURES OF LIGHTNING LUCY
THERE'S A PHARAOH IN OUR BATH!
THERE'S A VIKING IN MY BED AND OTHER STORIES
TROUBLE WITH ANIMALS

Read more about Streaker's adventures:
THE HUNDRED-MILE-AN-HOUR DOG
RETURN OF THE HUNDRED-MILE-AN-HOUR DOG
WANTED! THE HUNDRED-MILE-AN-HOUR DOG
LOST! THE HUNDRED-MILE-AN-HOUR DOG

Read more about Nicholas's daft family:
MY DAD'S GOT AN ALLIGATOR!
MY GRANNY'S GREAT ESCAPE
MY MUM'S GOING TO EXPLODE!
MY BROTHER'S FAMOUS BOTTOM
MY BROTHER'S FAMOUS BOTTOM GETS PINCHED
MY BROTHER'S FAMOUS BOTTOM GOES CAMPING
MY BROTHER'S HOT CROSS BOTTOM

Jeremy STRONG'S

LAUGH-YOUR-SOCKS-OFF

CLASSROOM CHAOS

Joke

Book

Starring: Miss Pandemonium, Captain Blackpatch and Siggy
the Viking. Did somebody say VIKING? Arrrrrrrrgggggggh!

PUFFIN

PUFFIN BOOKS

Published by the Penguin Group
Penguin Books Ltd, 80 Strand, London WC2R 0RL, England
Penguin Group (USA) Inc., 375 Hudson Street, New York, New York 10014, USA
Penguin Group (Canada), 90 Eglinton Avenue East, Suite 700, Toronto,
Ontario, Canada M4P 2Y3 (a division of Pearson Penguin Canada Inc.)
Penguin Ireland, 25 St Stephen's Green, Dublin 2, Ireland (a division of Penguin Books Ltd)
Penguin Group (Australia), 250 Camberwell Road, Camberwell, Victoria 3124, Australia
(a division of Pearson Australia Group Pty Ltd)
Penguin Books India Pvt Ltd, 11 Community Centre, Panchsheel Park,
New Delhi – 110 017, India
Penguin Group (NZ), 67 Apollo Drive, Rosedale, North Shore 0632, New Zealand
(a division of Pearson New Zealand Ltd)
Penguin Books (South Africa) (Pty) Ltd, 24 Sturdee Avenue, Rosebank,
Johannesburg 2196, South Africa

Penguin Books Ltd, Registered Offices: 80 Strand, London WC2R 0RL, England

puffinbooks.com

First published 2010
1

Copyright © Puffin Books, 2010
Introduction and short story copyright © Jeremy Strong, 2010
Illustrations copyright © Nick Sharratt, Judy Brown, Rowan Clifford, Ian Cunliffe, 2010
All rights reserved

The moral right of the author and illustrators has been asserted

Compiled and designed by Perfect Bound Ltd
Made and printed in England by Clays Ltd, St Ives plc

British Library Cataloguing in Publication Data
A CIP catalogue record for this book is available from the British Library

ISBN: 978–0–141–32799–0

www.greenpenguin.co.uk

Mixed Sources
Product group from well-managed
forests and other controlled sources
www.fsc.org Cert no. SA-COC-1592
© 1996 Forest Stewardship Council

Penguin Books is committed to a sustainable future
for our business, our readers and our planet.
The book in your hands is made from paper
certified by the Forest Stewardship Council.

Contents

Introduction

Ah, school. Love it or hate it, you have to go. Even if you turn into a dinosaur overnight, you have to go. Even if you want to be a pirate, you have to go. And you have to go for 190 days a year, for at least thirteen years ... wow, that makes almost 2,500 days! Crikey.

Of course, lots of those will be good days. You'll have a favourite teacher, a fun lesson, a trip out, some snow in the playground. But other days might be a bit boring. On those days, you need something to cheer you up. A few jokes. Some tricks and games to play would be good. Oh, hang on a second ... Here they are, right in your hand! Gosh, how lucky is that?

Oops, there goes the bell – we're late! Quick, run and line up. See you inside.

Lesson One: English

There's not a lot to say about English. You're reading this, so you've probably got the hang of the basics. You may not be up to the level of words like triskaidekaphobia or steatopygous*, but you can read and write OK.

Make the most of reading. Do it as much as you can. Because (and here's the science bit) the more you read, the bigger your brain gets. How cool is that? Not that you'll get a big swollen head, just that your brain will get more wrinkly and joined up inside. Which will help in pretty much everything you do.

However, writing poems about days of the week does you absolutely no good at all.

Why did Tigger spend so long in the loo?
He was looking for Pooh.

*Triskaidekaphobia: fear of the number 13. Steatopygous: with a really big bottom. I have no idea how you *say* them.

What's a witch's favourite subject? **Spelling.**

Sherlock Holmes was reading when Watson came running in, looking confused.

'I say, Holmes!' he exclaimed. 'Why on earth have you painted our front door bright yellow?'

'Lemon-entry, my dear Watson,' came the reply.

'Mr Dedman says that when you have finished, you can have two minutes to write a poem.'

'A whole poem? Two minutes?' asked Harry Franklin. 'Can we choose our own subject?'

'I'm afraid not,' answered Mrs Dove. 'You know Mr Dedman always likes to choose the subject. The title is "Wednesday".'

'Wednesday.' What a brilliant title – and a whole two minutes to write about it too, *if* you could possibly think of anything to say about 'Wednesday'.

Chicken School

Turn over to see Tim's poem!

What's the difference between a boring teacher and a boring book? **You can shut the book up.**

Dad, I got an A in spelling!

You idiot! There isn't an A in 'spelling'!

I bet I can say the alphabet faster than you.

Bet you can't.

'The alphabet' – beat you!

I've accidentally swallowed a dictionary!

Don't breathe a word to anybody.

4

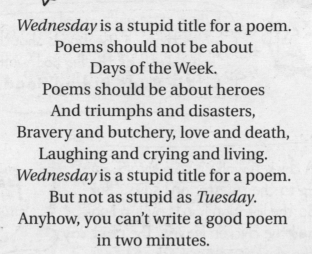

Wednesday is a stupid title for a poem.
Poems should not be about
Days of the Week.
Poems should be about heroes
And triumphs and disasters,
Bravery and butchery, love and death,
Laughing and crying and living.
Wednesday is a stupid title for a poem.
But not as stupid as *Tuesday*.
Anyhow, you can't write a good poem
in two minutes.

Chicken School

How do you spell 'hungry horse'
with just four letters?
MT GG.

How many mystery writers does
it take to change a light bulb?
**Two. One to screw it
almost all the way in, and
one to give it a surprising
twist at the end.**

Which little girl in a red cape walks through the woods shouting 'bumcakes!' at the Big Bad Wolf? **Little Rude Riding Hood.**

A chicken walks into a library, goes up to the counter and says, 'Buk.' So the librarian hands over a book and the chicken leaves. The next day the chicken comes back and says, 'Buk-buk.' So the librarian holds out two books. The chicken tucks one under each wing, and walks out. The next day the chicken comes in again and says, 'Buk-buk-buk.' The librarian helps her to three books, but is desperate to find out why the chicken wants them, so she follows the chicken out of the library, down the road to the river. She watches as the chicken takes the books to the riverbank, where a frog is sitting. As the chicken holds up each book in turn, the frog says, 'Reddit. Reddit. Reddit.'

I thought I'd tell you the story of the three holes in the ground. You haven't heard it? **Well, well, well.**

What does Giant Jim like to read? **Tall tales.**

What is a twack? **What a twain runs on.**

If can't is short for cannot, what is don't short for? **Doughnut.**

Give me a sentence using the word 'benign'.

This year, I be eight — but next year I benign.

Dad walked into a cafe with a lizard on his shoulder and ordered. 'I'll have a cup of tea, and Tiny here would like an orange juice.'
'Why do you call your lizard Tiny?' asked the waitress.
'Because he's my newt.'

An Eskimo was paddling through the Arctic sea in his kayak when he started to get really cold. To try to get warm, he lit a fire on top of his boat. Sadly, the fire burned the kayak and he fell in the water. So he learned a useful lesson: you can't have your kayak and heat it.

If a writer can write, and a teacher can teach, why can't a finger fing?

Mum always makes omelettes with two eggs, but when we're on holiday in France, she only uses one. That's because in France, one egg is **un oeuf!**

Deer Post Offisss
We hav got your postman.
Giv us a millyon ponds
or you wont get him bak
EVER !!!
Singed: The Indoor Pirates
Bald Ben xxx   Captin Blackpatch
x x x   Lumpy Lawsoxn
Molly → Polly
Me ↑ not her! ← Me ↑ not her!

'Now, all we have to do is send this letter to
the Post Office,' chuckled Captain Blackpatch.
'Soon we shall be as rich as kings!'

The postman got to his feet and smiled at
everyone. 'As it happens, I was just on
my way to the Post Office. I'll take the
letter with me if you like.'

Captain Blackpatch was
overcome. 'You are kind.
What a jolly nice postman
you are. Thank you so
much. You will deliver it
safely, won't you?'

'Of course,' said the
postman. 'That's my job.'

The Indoor Pirates

Have you ever wondered why English is so hard to learn? Here's one reason: a sentence containing eight different ways of pronouncing 'ough'.

I thought I saw the rough, dough-faced ploughboy cough and hiccough his way through the borough.

(Hiccough is an old-fashioned way of spelling hiccup.)

Anagrams

Have you played with anagrams? Rearranging the letters in a word or phrase can sometimes reveal something. For instance . . .

ASTRONOMER = MOON STARER.
THE EYES = THEY SEE.
THE MORSE CODE = HERE COMES DOT.
A DECIMAL POINT = I'M A DOT IN PLACE.
ELEVEN PLUS TWO = TWELVE PLUS ONE.

What could you make from the letters in your name?

There's just time before the end of the lesson to choose a new reading book. Let's see what's left on the shelf:

Singalong Fun by Carrie Oakey

When's Your Birthday? By Anna Versary

Walking on the Cliffs by Eileen Dover

I Love Chips by Zoltan Vinegar

Banging Tunes by Drummond Base

Sorry They've Gone by Emma Fred-Knott

They Were Lovely by Arthur N. E. More

Just What I Wanted by Chris Mass-Present

Chocolate Treats by E. Streg

I Met Dracula by Drew Bludd

A Pair of Comics by Dan Dee and Bea Know

Education Confusion

Oh no, the timetable's got mixed up!
Can you work out which
lesson is which?

RAT
. . . .

SHINGLE
. . . .

HIRTOYS
. . . .

SHMAT
. . . .

PARGOHYGE
. . . .

SICEENC
. . . .

TROPS
. . . .

SUMIC
. . . .

Answers on page 136

Pupil Assessment for:
Polly – no, Molly. I think.

English: Polly (or possibly Molly) shows great enthusiasm for creative writing. However she (they?) needs/need to work on her/their spelling and grammar. And handwriting.

Mathematics: Molly (Polly?) likes large numbers, especially 1,000,000. In fact, this tends to be her answer to almost any question.

Geography: Polly and Molly love maps, though they need to stop drawing Xs on them and tearing them out of the textbooks.

Sport: The girls have excellent physical skills, especially on the ropes and bars. They are rather aggressive in the team games if they are on opposing sides. Actually, if they're on the same side they're even worse.

Excuses

Mrs Bolton sent Jodie into school with a note for her teacher.

'Dear Mrs Farouk,

Jodie turned into a dinosaur last night, but she seems quite well in herself. My husband has made an appointment for her to see the doctor, just in case. The big bunch of flowers is her lunch. She seems to prefer daisies.

Yours sincerely,

Mrs Bolton.'

Dinosaur Pox

Why are you crawling into school? And you're ten minutes late!

Well, miss, you said you didn't want to see me walking in late again.

I put my shoes on the wrong feet. And then I couldn't remember whose feet I'd put them on.

Where's your homework?

It blew out of my hand on the way to school.

I see. And why are you late?

I had to wait ages for the wind to get strong enough.

I'm sorry I'm late. I had a dream about a football match, and it went into extra time.

You should have been here at 9 o'clock!

Why, what happened?

Hello, is that the school? I'm afraid Nicholas won't be in today.

I'm sorry to hear that. Is he unwell?

Yes, he's very sick.

And who am I speaking to?

My dad.

Mum told me to put a clean pair of socks on every day, but when it got to Friday I couldn't get my shoes on.

I'm sorry Rob was absent from school yesterday; he had a bad cold. He will also have a cold next Thursday and Friday.

Lesson Two: Mathematics

Sometimes maths makes your brain feel like it's full of glue. But there is always an answer in maths and a good teacher can show different people different ways to work out the same problem.

A lot of grown-ups seem to be quite proud of being no good at maths. Which is a bit weird. I mean, you'd never hear anyone laugh and say, 'Oh, don't ask me to read! I'm rubbish at reading! Absolutely useless. Never bothered to learn – always hated it.' If you hear someone showing off about how rubbish they are at maths, remember not to lend them any money.

Which word of five letters has six left when you take two away? Sixty.

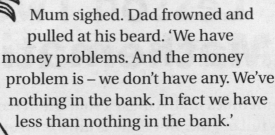

Mum sighed. Dad frowned and pulled at his beard. 'We have money problems. And the money problem is – we don't have any. We've nothing in the bank. In fact we have less than nothing in the bank.'

'Dad, how can you have less than nothing?' I asked.

'It's called an overdraft, Nicholas,' Lancelot explained. 'It means your mum and dad owe the bank money.'

My Brother's Famous Bottom

All our bills have gone up – food, gas, electricity, phone. Why can't anything ever go down?

You'll be pleased to see my homework marks then.

Why was six afraid of seven? **Because seven ate nine.**

Are you any good at maths?

Yes and no.

What do you mean?

Yes, I'm no good at maths.

How to prove that a pound is the same as a penny!

£1 = 100p
So £1 = 10p x 10p
So £1 = £0.1 x £0.1
So £1 = £0.01
So £1 = 1p

If I cut three apples, four oranges and two pears into ten pieces each, what will I have?
A tasty fruit salad.

Knock, knock.

Who's there?

Six times seven is forteet.

Six times seven is forteet who?

Wow, you're good at maths.

'Amy, what is six hundred and ninety-two, add five thousand two hundred and sixty, divided by eight?'

It was Amy's turn to groan. That was hopelessly hard to do in her head. 'Don't know, miss,' she whispered, and waited for a scream of anger.

'Neither do I,' smiled Miss Pandemonium. 'But it must be an awful lot. Well then, that's got our maths done for the day. What do we do next?'

Pandemonium at School

A butcher is 1.82 metres tall and has size 13 feet. What does he weigh? **Sausages.**

Pick a number. Add twenty. Take away three. Multiply by ten. Now close your eyes. Done that?

Yes.

Dark, isn't it?

If you had five potatoes, how would you share them between three people?

Mash them.

What's a polygon? **A dead parrot.**

Which king invented fractions?
Henry the $\frac{1}{8}$.

How many people can stand on an empty football pitch?
One — after that, it isn't empty.

How old are you, Sue?

I'm nine.

I see. And what are you going to be when you're older?

Ten.

A girl went into a baker's. 'How much are the doughnuts?' she asked.
'Two for 50p,' the baker replied. 'Or 30p for one.'
'Then I'll take the other one for 20p,' said the girl.

I asked you to write about what you'd do if you had a million pounds. Why have you handed in a blank sheet of paper? You've written nothing!

Because that's what I'd do if I had a million pounds, miss — nothing.

What did the zero say to the eight? **Nice belt!**

'Well,' declared the king. 'How you've grown!' Belinda nodded. 'I hear you've been taught a great deal over the last seven years.'

'Yes, Father,' said Belinda gently.

'Hmmm. Very useful thing, knowledge. So – you've learnt lots and lots. Well now, tell me, um, what are three sixes?'

Belinda shrugged. 'I don't know.'

'You don't know!' King Stormbelly was cross. He had hoped she would be able to tell him because he didn't know the answer himself.

The Karate Princess

Dad, can you help me find the lowest common denominator?

I remember that from when I was at school. So they still haven't found it yet then?

These new glasses I've bought you are really expensive, OK?
So I don't want you to wear them when you're not looking at anything.

If you had £3.50 in one pocket and £2.20 in the other pocket, what would you have?

Someone else's trousers on, miss.

Do you know the best way to save money?
Forget who you borrowed it from.

Have you had your maths homework marked yet?

Yes. I'm afraid you didn't do very well.

Struggling with your maths homework? **Call the Maths Helpline on 0800 (10x)(13i)-2 cos(xy)² /2.362**

What's the difference between wages and a salary, sir?

Well, if you get paid wages, you get paid every week, but if you get paid a salary, you get paid every month. For example, I get a salary and I'm paid every month.

Really? Where do you work, sir?

What's the quickest way to double your money? **Fold it in half.**

What is half of eight?

That depends. Up and down, or across?

What do you mean?

Well, up and down is a three; going across you get a zero.

My dad says there are three types of people in the world: those that can do maths, and those that can't.

Creature Count

How many animals has Nicholas got living with him now?

Answers on page 136

Pupil Assessment for:
Nicholas

Mathematics: Nicholas does much better work in class than in his homework. He handed in a recent worksheet about money that was extremely disappointing. Perhaps his father could stop 'helping' Nicholas.

English: Nicholas shows an extremely vivid imagination. He needs to learn to be more realistic in his factual writing, however. His diary recently has been simply unbelievable.

Science: Nicholas has a good knowledge of the habits and appetites of many animals. Suspiciously good, actually; how on earth does he know so much about crocodiles?

Music: Nicholas shows some ability, but he needs to get over his reluctance about singing in public. I'm not sure what is putting him off, as he has a good voice.

Lesson Three: History

History may seem to be only about boring old things that happened a long time ago, but think about it. When these wars and plagues and beheadings were actually happening, it was probably quite exciting. Everything that's happening now, here, today, is going to turn into history some day. All you have to do is wait a bit.

Why didn't they send postcards in the Stone Age?
Have you ever tried sticking a stamp to a rock?

What happened when the wheel was invented?
It started a revolution.

Which queen burped the most?
Queen Hic-toria.

I wish I'd been born a thousand years ago.
Just think of all the history I wouldn't have to learn.

'Good morning,' cried Mr Ellis, flashing his best smile. 'You must be Mrs Tibblethwaite. You've arrived early.'

'Good morning,' replied the lady stonily. 'I always arrive early. You must be the Viking Hotel.'

'I'm Mr Ellis. Did you have a good journey?'

'No . . . we went to the Viking cafe, the Viking Restaurant, The Viking's Delight, The Viking Chinese Take-away and The Viking Burgerbar.'

'Well, you're here now,' smiled Mr Ellis, seizing the heavy suitcase. 'Follow me, and I'll show you to your room.'

'Just why are there so many Viking places around here?' asked Mrs Tibblethwaite, stomping up the stairs behind Mr Ellis.

'Ah, well, over a thousand years ago, Flotby was a favourite target for the Viking raiders from Denmark.'

There's a Viking in my Bed

How does Siggy send messages?
By Norse Code.

 Which queen was the fattest?
Mary, Queen of Scones.

What does the Queen do when she burps?
She issues a royal pardon.

 Where were most British kings and queens crowned?
On their heads.

How was the Roman Empire divided in two?
With a pair of Caesars.

 In the Sixties, what did hippies do?
They held your leggies on to your body.

Can you name something special that didn't exist 100 years ago?

Me!

Robin Hood was dying when he called out to his friend, 'Little John, Little John – bring me my trusty bow.' Little John brought him the bow. Then Robin Hood asked, 'Little John, Little John – bring me my trusty arrow.' So Little John did as he asked. Robin Hood notched the arrow, drew back his bow and with his final breath said, 'Wherever this arrow lands, there let me be buried.' So they buried him on top of the wardrobe.

What did Alexander the Great have in common with Winnie the Pooh?
They had the same middle name.

Who made King Arthur's round table?
Sir Cumference.

One of the things we did in History at school was learn about the sort of homes posh people lived in two or three hundred years ago, and one of the things they did was paint pictures all over their ceilings. They didn't paint them themselves of course because they were posh. They got other people, some not-at-all-posh people, to do the painting for them. Mrs Fetlock took our class on a trip to Bling House – 'So you can see how civilized people lived,' she explained. 'People who knew how to handle a knife and fork properly,' she added, eyeing Megan Morgan very coldly.

Beware! Killer Tomatoes

Why did Henry VIII have so many wives?
He liked to chop and change.

What did Napoleon become on his 41st birthday?
A year older.

Then it was Ben's turn again. 'When Pharaohs were mummified, the priests cut out the lungs, liver, and other stomach bits and put them into, well, sort of jam-jars.'

'There's no need to go into detail,' said Mr Lightspeed, green-faced. 'We haven't had breakfast yet.'

'Well, they did,' Ben went on. 'They had to get the brain out too and that was *really* difficult. They'd get a long piece of wire with a hook on one end and pull your brain out down your nostrils –'

'BEN!'

'All I'm saying *is*: how come Sennapod can wander around if all his insides are missing and he's got no brain?'

There's a Pharaoh in our Bath!

How can you tell when Sennapod is angry?
He flips his lid.

How does a mummy's doorbell work?
Toot and come in.

Sennapod Shadows

Match the right shadow to each of these pictures of Sennapod.

Answers on page 136

Pupil Assessment:
Sennapod, Lord of Serpents, Master of Hippos and Crusher of Worms

History: Sennapod has been an *interesting* addition to the class. Sometimes I imagine he must live in a museum, he knows so much!

Science: Sennapod is very good with animals, especially cats. He's less good with humans.

English: Considering English is not his first language, Sennapod is remarkably fluent – especially in his insults, which can be almost amusing. He needs to work on his handwriting.

Art: Sennapod has a natural talent for art. He loves to draw beautiful rows of animals and people, though he gets quite upset when we can't 'read' them.

Form teacher's remarks: Sennapod needs to work on his attitude to authority. Basically, he has too much of it. I would also remind him that make-up is not permitted in school.

classroom chaos

Part One

A Noisy and Dangerous Triangle, With Feet

Dee-doo dee-doo dee-doo! What was that? Was it the police rushing off to arrest a bank robber? Were the fire brigade racing down the street chasing a burning car?

No. It was just Miss Pandemonium on her way to school, driving her old ambulance. It really had been a real ambulance many years ago, but now it was Miss Pandemonium's ambulance and she found it very useful to use her siren.

A school had just rung her. 'This is Crackpot Primary School. The head teacher Mrs Snorkel says can you come straight away? One of our teachers has been taken ill and there is nobody to look after Class Five.'

So Miss Pandemonium quickly jumped into her ambulance and just as quickly jumped back out of it.

'Oh dear. I've forgotten my handbag.' She rushed indoors and rushed back out, leaped into the ambulance and leaped out again.

'I've forgotten my hairbrush. Can't have messy hair.' She dashed back indoors and dashed back out, flung herself into the ambulance and flung herself back out.

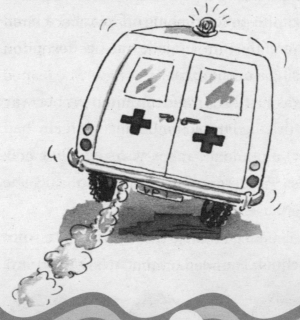

'And I must have a potted plant on my desk – then I shall feel at home.' So she grabbed a potted plant, dived into her ambulance and this time she was off, with a great scrunching of gears and squealing of tyres.

Skrrrrrkkkk! Vrooooom!! Dee-doo dee-doo!!!

Cars skidded out of her path. Trucks screeched to a halt. People scattered like pigeons to get out of her way. And pigeons squawked and flapped like *very* annoyed people. In fact everyone got in a flap when Miss Pandemonium was out and about.

Everyone, except Miss Pandemonium, who raced along wearing a great big smile. She pulled into the car park of Crackpot Primary School, siren blaring and almost drove right into the reception area but skidded to a halt just in time! She leaped out, flowerpot tucked under one arm, bag over the other, and ran into the school.

'I'm Miss Pandemonium,' she announced. 'Supply Teacher. Class Five need rescuing. Show me the way!'

'WHO is making that DREADFUL noise?!' a voice bellowed. Miss Pandemonium whirled round.

Coming towards her was a very small woman with a very loud voice. She was short and round, with a tiny head, large bosom and fat legs. Basically, she looked like a triangle. A very noisy triangle. With feet.

'Hello!' beamed Miss Pandemonium. 'I'm the supply teacher. I've come to –'

'I know perfectly well why you're here. I am the head teacher, Mrs Snorkel. Was that you making that dreadful noise?'

'Dreadful noise? Me?' Miss Pandemonium looked rather confused and patted herself all over as if some part of her might have made an unpleasant sound. A large crowd of quietly sniggering children had gathered behind Mrs Snorkel.

'Not you yourself,' cried Mrs Snorkel. 'I mean – YOU! Doing things!'

'Doing things?' repeated Miss Pandemonium. 'Was I doing things? What sort of things? Cart-wheels? No, that wasn't me. Burps? Oh, I hope not. I didn't burp, did I ? I do sometimes, by mistake, but never in public. Do tell me I didn't burp.'

Mrs Snorkel was pulling at her hair, her nose, her ears and her chin in exasperation. 'What kind of idiotic twaddle are you talking about now, woman? I was in the middle of a very important assembly and I was interrupted by the most frightful wailing and squealing from outside. I looked through the doors and saw an ambulance hurtling into the reception area. And then – YOU!'

'Ah yes,' smiled Miss Pandemonium. 'Me! I'm here!'

'We all know that,' Mrs Snorkel growled in a voice that was so low and heavy it was practically crawling across the ground. 'Kindly go to Class Five's room and see to them. And please do it WITHOUT a wail, a squeak or a squawk.'

Miss Pandemonium beamed back at the head

teacher. 'How about a squook?' she suggested, and the children behind Mrs Snorkel sniggered even more.

'GO!' roared the head teacher.

Miss Pandemonium didn't bat an eyelid. She gazed steadily back at the red-faced head. 'I think your assembly children are waiting for you,' she said quietly. Then she turned and went off, whistling a happy tune.

Miss Pandemonium found Class Five at the end of a long corridor. In fact she heard them before she saw them. It sounded as if a small riot was taking place. She pushed open the door just in time to see a large paper dart sail serenely across the classroom and make a crash-landing on Lily's head.

'Oh,' said Lily. 'I seem to have a new hat.'

'It suits you,' smiled Miss Pandemonium. 'Everyone, please stand up.'

Chairs and tables scraped as the whole class got to their feet. Miss Pandemonium nodded and told them all to sit down again.

'Why did we have to stand up?' asked Tyler.

'I wanted to see how tall you were,' Miss

Pandemonium answered.

'Why?' Tyler went on.

'Just in case,' Miss Pandemonium said.

'In case of what?' Tyler pressed her.

Miss Pandemonium looked straight at him. 'In case I have to cut you down to size,' she replied. The rest of the class giggled quietly while Tyler muttered darkly to himself. 'Huh. She's weird, she is.'

'Now then,' their new teacher went on. 'My name is Miss Pandemonium. I shall be looking after you until your usual teacher is better.' She gazed round the room. The walls were empty. She couldn't see a single piece of work – no writing, no pictures, just paint.

'Your classroom looks a bit bare,' she observed.

'Mrs Snorkel says pictures just make clutter. She doesn't like clutter,' Wesley offered.

'And she says our writing work isn't good enough to be put on display,' said Katie. 'Megan won a poetry-writing competition in a newspaper last month and Mrs Snorkel says even that isn't good enough because her poem was funny and it was about a hippopotamus and Mrs Snorkel says funny poems aren't worth the bother and she doesn't like animals anyway and hippos are fat and horrible.'

'Really?' murmured Miss Pandemonium. 'In that case we had better see if we can change things. Would you like to have pictures on the walls?'

'Oh yes!' half the class cried.

'And your writing too?'

'Brilliant!' yelled the other half.

A lone voice piped up. It was a small boy with a mouse-like face. 'What sort of writing?' he asked.

'Well, I thought it might be fun to write about animals. After all, if Katie can write a prize-winning poem about a hippopotamus I'm sure the rest of you can do just as well. You look like a pretty clever bunch to me.'

The children were immediately buzzing with ideas, except for Katie, who wasn't sure that she wanted the rest of the class to be as good as her. Even so – writing about animals, and drawing them too! That would be fantastic.

The rest of the day passed with hardly a peep from Class Five. Tables became crammed with books on tigers and apes, dragonflies and eagles, ants and penguins and elephants and seals and mosquitoes. Writing poured out of the children. It was as if a huge dam had burst. Questions were hurled at their new teacher.

'How should I write my poem about a shark?' asked Tyler.

'Write it how you want it to be,' advised Miss Pandemonium. So Tyler wrote it how he wanted it and he wanted it with a different colour for each word he put down. It took a long time to write but it looked very colourful when he had finished and he was proud of it.

'That's terrific,' beamed Miss Pandemonium. 'I like the way you've used a lot of red when the shark catches the poor head teacher and eats her. Does it have to be a head teacher that the shark eats?'

'Oh yes,' declared Tyler. 'Because, you see, it's a Head Teacher-Eating Shark. It only eats head teachers.'

'In that case I must make sure I never become a head teacher,' smiled Miss Pandemonium.

Paint was pulled out of the cupboard for the first time. Brushes were discovered. Huge sheets of paper were spread across tables and the floor. Paint began to flow and soon pictures were being stuck on to the wall.

By the end of the day they were all exhausted, but the classroom had changed beyond measure. The children looked at the walls and grinned at each other.

'I think we are doing very well,' said Miss Pandemonium. 'Now then, it's almost time to go home. I understand that tomorrow our class has to

give an assembly to the whole school. I want you to bring cardboard boxes, as many as you can get hold of. And it doesn't matter what size they are – in fact the bigger the better.'

'What do we need so many boxes for, miss?' asked Maya.

Miss Pandemonium winked at her. 'Wait and see. There's something else I would like you to bring too.' Miss Pandemonium checked carefully to make sure nobody else could hear. She gathered her class in closer and told them what she was after.

Their eyes bulged. Their jaws almost fell on the floor.

'But, miss,' began Sunil, 'Mrs Snorkel says –'

'Sssh,' interrupted Miss Pandemonium. 'I take full responsibility, so please see what you can do.' And don't tell ANYONE. It's our secret.' Miss Pandemonium beamed at them all and the children went off home, chatting excitedly to each other.

'It's been the best day ever,' said Jennie.

'It won't last,' warned Harry. 'You know what Mrs Snorkel is like. She'll tear down the paintings and our poems and stuff. She's bound to come and see sooner or later and then we'll all be in for it. Especially Miss Pandemonium. Mrs Snorkel will tear her limb from limb and bury her at the bottom of the school field. You wait and see.'

What will happen next?
Is Mrs Snorkel going to
go on the rampage?

Turn to page 88 to find out!

Lesson Four: ICT

It's weird to think that computers have only been in schools for about ten to fifteen years. These days it seems you can't do anything without them – yet human beings seemed to manage without them for, oh, thousands of years. Weird.

The PC was born in 1981; the worldwide web was born in 1990. In 1993 there were only 600 websites in the entire world. Can you imagine what computing will be like in ten years' time? Twenty years? Fifty years? When you're a wrinkly, will you be boring your grandchildren – 'Oooh, I remember when you had to carry the web around in a little box, with a battery in it, and sometimes you couldn't get a signal . . .'?

Things change fast. So no more moaning about how old the school computers are.

Where does a prawn meet his girlfriend?
On the net.

Miss, I just pushed some roast pork in the computer.

That was silly. Is it broken?

No, but there's a lot of crackling.

What instructions did Father Christmas give to use his computer? **First, yule log on . . .**

We had IT first thing on Monday. There was one computer room that served the whole school and, since we were first in that morning, we had to switch on and get things going.

Mr Dedman had designed a welcome page for the school computer system. It also acted as a screen saver and basically it was a photo of the school that moved slowly round the screen, along with the words:

Welcome to Peasewood Junior School

It was a triumph of Dedhead's imagination.

Chicken School

Why on earth have you painted black and white squares all over the monitor?

I wanted to check my email.

Gran hasn't got the hang of shopping on the Internet. **Her trolley keeps falling off the computer.**

Why did the chicken cross the web? **To get to the other site.**

How many computer programmers does it take to change a light bulb? **None, they won't do it — it's a hardware problem.**

'Does this computer have a copier?'

'A what?'

'A copier, you know, for copying things.'

'Oh! You mean like a photocopier?'

Norman gave me a weird look, as if I was truly stupid. 'Of course not, Jellyhead,' he sneered. 'I mean like copying living things. Dogs, cats, elephants . . .'

'You've got a computer that can do that?'

Inside, you can bet my mind was going boggle-boggle, but I tried to stay calm. This was like an actual admission. I mean, short of him actually saying 'I am an alien,' this was it!

But Norman was getting bored. He seemed to think that my computer was hopelessly out of date. 'My dad's in computers,' he said. 'He knows more about computers than anyone in the universe.'

I'm Telling You, They're ALIENS!

How did the princess find out Rumpelstiltskin's name? **She checked his gnome page.**

Where do snowmen go online?
The winternet.

Why have you got a ruler taped to the monitor?

Mum wants to know how long I'm online.

How do you stop a laptop battery running out?
Hide its trainers.

I spent the whole of last night on the computer.

Tonight you should use a bed, it'll be more comfortable.

I'm not sure about letting you repair the school computer.

Don't worry, in the whole time I've been doing this, I've only ever made one computer blow up.

Wow. So how many computers have you fixed?

This'll be the second.

Why shouldn't you let a penguin use your computer?
Because the chocolate melts all over the keyboard.

How did the keyboard get out of prison?
He used his escape key.

The old woman was sitting in a motorized wheelchair. She had built it herself, adapting an old tea-trolley. She sat on the top tray, like some strange, large cake, with legs dangling over the front. An electric motor took up most of the bottom tray. Arranged around her were all sorts of controls.

As for the desk, it was piled high with scissors and knives, reels of thread, needles, pins and rolls of sticky tape. Mixed in with all this was a jumble of electrics – small motors, TV tuners, wiring, hard-drives and umpteen other nerdy bits from cannibalized computers.

Krankenstein's Crazy House of Horror

I have a spelling checker
It came with my PC.
It plainly marks four my revue
Missed aches I cannot sea.
I've run this poem threw it,
I'm sure your please to no.
It's letter perfect in its way;
My checker tolled me sew.

How do you know when a stupid person has used your computer?
Tippex on the screen.

Why is a tiger like a computer?
They've both got mega-bites.

Whatismoreannoyingthana keyboardwithastuckspacebar?
A beykoard wiht some of hte beys spawwed over.

I crossed my laptop with an elephant.
Now it's got loads of memory, but I can't lift it.

Connect Two

Draw lines to join up pairs of words to make twelve new words that you will find in ICT.

SOFT	BOARD
DATA	LINE
KEY	BASE
BROAD	STICK
LAP	SITE
JOY	LOAD
MAIN	BAND
PASS	FRAME
WEB	TOP
DOWN	WARE
ON	WORD

Answers on page 136

Pupil Assessment:
Norman Vork

ICT: Norman's computer skills are remarkable, though I wish he wouldn't be so critical of the school's equipment. We do our best with limited resources – some items have gone missing recently.

Music: Norman struggles to appreciate music. I know some of our pupils need more practice (Rob Smith and his violin, for instance), but honestly. You'd think it actually hurt him to listen.

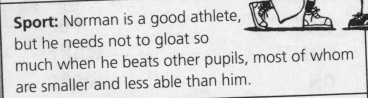

Sport: Norman is a good athlete, but he needs not to gloat so much when he beats other pupils, most of whom are smaller and less able than him.

Form teacher's notes: Norman joined the school halfway through the year and has had some trouble fitting in. Apparently his father's work means they move house often, and this may have affected his ability to make friends. He's very vague about where his family comes from, but I get the impression it's a long way away.

Lunchtime

School dinners used to be pretty awful, which is why grown-ups can tell you plenty of jokes and horror stories about what they had to eat.

Schools have to try a bit harder these days. The choices are healthier, and some of those choices may actually taste great. This is obviously a good thing. And you can ignore those tasty healthy choices and have the junk food, if you like.

Dinner ladies are great, though. They have to get specially trained to use that clicky scoop thing to serve mash and ice cream. Let's hope they wash it in between courses!

It's rock cakes for pudding, take your pick.

I don't need a pick, I need a hammer and chisel.

I think the cook has got a bit carried away with her new juicer. She served fish juice last Friday. With chip juice.

Yuck, there are two worms on my plate!

Stop complaining, those are the sausages.

We don't have to wait for a bell to say when it's lunchtime. We just listen for the smoke alarm.

I shook my head. 'Streaker's going to beat your dogs.'

'Oh, I don't think so,' crowed Charlie. 'She might beat one of them, but she won't beat all three, no way.' He poked my chest with a stubby, dirty finger. 'You're history, sunshine.'

'Yeah?' I bravely replied. 'Well if I'm history then you're . . . you're school dinners!'

That shut him up. It shut me up too! I don't think either of us had any idea what I was on about.

Return of the Hundred-Mile-An-Hour Dog

We've been given fish to eat so often that I'm beginning to breathe through my neck.

How do you make a sausage roll? **Push it down a hill.**

What do snowmen have for lunch? **Icebergers.**

This vinegar's got lumps in it!

Those are pickled onions.

Eat up your sprouts, they'll put colour in your cheeks.

Maybe, but who wants green cheeks?

This lunch tastes funny.

Well, why aren't you laughing?

Here you go, rhubarb crumble.

Why is this bowl a metre long?

I couldn't find any shorter rhubarb.

Our cook makes shortbread that melts in your mouth. It takes a few days, but eventually, it melts.

I got told off at lunchtime. It turns out 'a balanced diet' doesn't mean a bag of crisps in each hand.

The noisiest eater was the head teacher, Patagonia Clatterbottom. She sat in her boat-pram, eating a great pile of food. She had one big sausage, two fried eggs, three bits of bacon, and at least four hundred baked beans. SHLIPP! SHLURPP! BURRPP!

What were the children eating? Ziggy was eating a single baked bean. Corkella was eating a baked bean. Smudge and Flo were each eating a baked bean. Even Jazz the dog was eating a baked bean. It was a very small lunch.

'I'm hungry,' moaned Ziggy.

'We're all hungry,' grumbled Corkella.

'Woof,' said Jazz.

Pirate School: The Bun Gun

Do gooseberries have legs?

No, of course not.

Ah. Then I've just swallowed a caterpillar.

What do really clever people eat for lunch?

I don't know.

Hmm, no, I didn't think you would.

I don't like this cheese with holes in it.

Well, eat the cheese and leave the holes on the side of your plate.

Why are school cooks cruel? **Because they beat eggs and whip cream.**

What sits in custard looking cross? **Apple grumble.**

I snuck down there, only to run straight into one of the dinner ladies, Mrs Bevinson.

It's pretty easy to run into Mrs Bevinson because she's about three miles wide and made of old mattresses. Well, that's what she looks like, at any rate. Mrs Bevinson always walks very slowly, like a robot with a battery that's running down, her tiny, rolling-pin arms swinging at her sides. She's so wide she fills the school corridors like some minesweeper. I couldn't help but run straight into her.

Krazy Kow Saves the World – Well, Almost

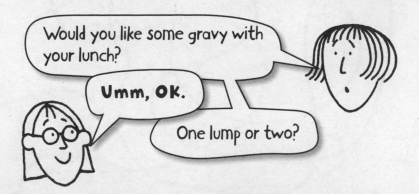

Would you like some gravy with your lunch?

Umm, OK.

One lump or two?

Lunch Lines

Which line will get Streaker to the plate of food?

Pupil Assessment: Streaker

Sport: Streaker has broken several school records, and even more school windows. Her speed is very impressive, but her stopping skills leave much to be desired.

Music: Streaker joins in eagerly, but her enthusiasm is not matched by her ability.

Art: I don't know what she did in the large vase I was making, but I can't get rid of the smell.

Form teacher's notes: Streaker needs to learn what is food and what isn't, and that we should only eat at lunchtimes. I was fond of that wallet. And those novelty rubbers. And those shoes.

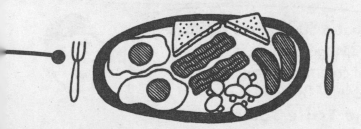

Lesson Five: Geography

Geography is the study of the Earth, and what happens on it. It's a huge subject, so don't get fed up when you get stuck colouring in maps. There's a lot more to discover. Geography is also one of the subjects you get to go on trips for, maybe even staying away from school. So that's a bonus. And if it means you can point out when the annoying sat-nav lady is about to direct your dad off a cliff, then you've really learned something.

What's red and green and hops around Australia?
Kanga-rhubarb.

What's 300 metres tall, made of sponge cake, fruit, custard and cream, and stands in the middle of Paris?
The Trifle Tower.

Can you tell me six animals you would find at the North Pole?

Five polar bears and a seal.

What is the capital of America?
A.

Where would you find the Andes?
At the end of my armies.

What gets stuck in a corner but can still travel round the world?
A stamp.

What was the largest island in the world before Australia was discovered?
Australia.

Where is Hadrian's Wall?

At the end of Hadrian's garden, miss.

Where are you from?

Portugal.

Really? Which part?

All of me.

Where do American cows live?
Moo York.

My mum is from Iceland and my dad is from Cuba.
So that makes me an ice cube.

If I'm standing at the North Pole, facing south, with the east on my left hand, what is on my right hand?

Fingers.

Tom Nunnery had drawn the treasure map, and he had tried to make it look as authentic as possible. Mrs Patel's classroom had 'Here be tiny people' written across it, while Mr Kuddle's office was called 'Cave of the Big Chief'. Above Class Six it said 'Beware of the Dragon', and there was a big black cross showing that the treasure was buried in the corner of the cave.

The treasure seekers were not terribly good at map-reading, and it took them quite a while to get their bearings and work out what Tom's strange clues meant. They walked round the hall four times. 'Trouble is,' muttered Tracey, 'you can't tell which way round this map goes. Who are the little people, anyway? I reckon Samantha's just playing tricks on us.'

Pirate Pandemonium

She smiled again and spoke in a throaty, foreign voice, making her r's growl.

'Come, Mr Vetman, sit down, you have had shock . . .'

'I'm still having one,' Dad murmured.

'Make custard.' This was Dinah the Mynah. Sometimes she gets words stuck in her tiny brain and keeps repeating them.

'My name – Miriana. I from Romania. I nice lady like it say here.' Miriana pointed to the advert. 'Now I make you cup of coffee and I stay and I look after you and this little man and everyone is happy. No?'

Little man! Honestly, she made me sound like a garden gnome!

The Beak Speaks

What's the fastest country in the world?
Russia.

Have you ever seen a duchess?

Yes, it was the same as an English S.

Why is Europe like a frying pan?
Because it has Greece at the bottom.

Knock, knock!

Who's there?

Norway.

Norway who?

Norway am I doing any more of these terrible jokes.

If someone from Poland is a Pole, what do you call someone from Holland?
A Hole.

What do Eskimoes use to hold their houses together?
Ig glue.

'Tell us all about life in Hedeby, Sigurd.'

'Hedeby – my town. Lots of Vikings: some big like me, some small like baby, some young like Tim, some old like Crumble . . .'

'Rumble!' snapped Mr Rumble. 'And I'm not that old either, if you don't mind. What did you eat?'

Sigurd closed his eyes and licked his lips. 'Sometimes we have big feet,' he said. 'Very big feet to praise Thor, God of Thunder.'

'He means feast,' whispered Tim to the rest of the class, who were beginning to giggle.

'We eat chickens and pigs and sheep and coats.'

'Sheep and goats,' muttered Tim.

Viking at School

Pupil assessment:
Sigurd Tibblethwaite

Geography: Siggy has been very, *very* eager to learn since he arrived. His particular area of interest is the North Sea. He knows a lot about the countries that border it, but is rather vague about how to get from one place to another. He seems to think travel happens by magic!

English: Siggy is Danish, but he is enthusiastic and his knowledge of English is increasing. He gets rather mixed up with his vocabulary, but the Ellis family are being very supportive of his attempts to communicate . . . most of the time.

History: Siggy's eye-witness accounts of Viking life have been absolutely fascinating. However, in future I must ask that he leave Nosepicker (his sword) at home.

Form teacher's notes: Siggy is large for his age (he is more than 1,000) and rather clumsy. As a result I must insist that he practise his wrestling moves in his spare time, not at school. I enclose my latest dry-cleaning bill.

Cracking Crossword

Answer these questions about Siggy the mad Viking to complete the crossword.

Across

4   Who is the Viking god of thunder?

5   Which country does Siggy come from?

8   What is the last name of the woman Siggy marries?

10   What does Siggy have sticking out from his helmet?

Down

1   What is the name of Siggy's sword?

2   What is the name of Siggy's home village?

3   What sport does Siggy turn out to be rather good at?

6   What business do Tim and Zoe's parents run?

7   Where does Siggy end up in England?

9   What is Tim and Zoe's last name?

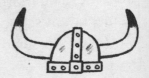

77

Answers on page 136

School Trip Bingo

Before we went on the trip Miss had to check all the biscuits in our packed lunches. She was doing a rusk assessment.

Next time you go on a school trip, take this page with you. Keep your eyes open and whenever one of these things happens to someone, cross it off the grid. If you get everything on the grid, shout BINGO!

Forgot the trip was happening	Wore the wrong clothes	Ate all their packed lunch on the coach	Threw up on the coach
Got lost	Called the teacher 'Mum'*	Learned a new rhyme	Walked in pairs holding hands
Teacher got stressed and shouted	Asked a really stupid question	Brought enough packed lunch for four people	Needed a wee at a really awkward time
Had a little cry	Had a food fight	Fell asleep on the way back	Had no idea what we learned, but it was fun!

* Doesn't count if the teacher really is their mum

Lesson Six: Science

If you thought geography was a big subject, you'll be scared of science. Science is the study of absolutely everything.

Well, sort of. It's the study of everything we can see, from massive galaxies to tiny atoms, including human and animal behaviour. Scientists look at things and try to work out why they happen the way they do.

Once a scientist comes up with an explanation for something (called a theory), other scientists check to see if it really works. They repeat the experiments, or look for things that don't fit the theory. If they find a single instance that doesn't agree with the theory, then the theory can't be right. If all the evidence supports the theory, then it's *probably* true.

That doesn't mean everyone will believe it, though!

What are microwaves?
What fleas do when they say goodbye.

How can you stop milk going sour?
Keep it in the cow.

How fast does light travel?

I don't know, miss — but it gets here far too early in the morning.

Which moves faster, heat or cold?
Heat. You can catch cold.

What scientific instrument do you use to serve tiny portions of ice cream?
A microscoop.

A scientist has just invented an amazing new liquid that can burn through anything. Now he's trying to invent something to keep it in.

My mouthwash says it kills 99.9% of all germs.

Yuck! That means your mouth is full of lots of dead germs.

What grows in a pod and can cut through steel?
A laser bean.

What happened when the light broke the law?
It was sent to prism.

Which is more useful, the sun or the moon?
The moon, because it helpfully shines at night when it's dark. The sun only shines in the day when it's light anyway.

'It's boiling, miss,' said Darren.

'Oh! So it is.' Miss Pandemonium turned from the clean blackboard, switched off the cooker and removed the can from the heat. She picked up the screw top and carefully screwed the lid on to the can. Then she put it on her desk and, without a word, began to unpack some of her bits and pieces. Even Samantha Boggis and her gang now had their eyes fixed on the can. What on earth was this weird woman doing?

Nothing happened, and then just as Class Five were beginning to get restless once again, there was a loud CLUNK, and one wall of the tin can bent inwards.

Pirate Pandemonium

What's the quickest way to blow up a balloon?
Dynamite.

What does a nuclear scientist have for lunch?
Fission chips.

How far can you see on a clear day? **93 million miles — all the way to the sun.**

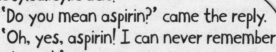

A chemist walks into a pharmacy and asks, 'Have you got any acetylsalicylic acid?'

'Do you mean aspirin?' came the reply.

'Oh, yes, aspirin! I can never remember that word.'

Little Willie was a chemist
Little Willie is no more
What he thought was H_2O
Was H_2SO_4

Apparently our sun is really a star. But luckily it knows how to turn back into a sun during the daytime.

Taking part in the environmental competition was Mrs Drew's idea. She's our head teacher. She's a great one for Saving the Planet. You should see her car. She's got this tiny little thing that she drives around. It does a million miles to a gallon of petrol, she says. In fact, I don't think it has an engine at all. I think that each tyre has got one of those rotating hamster wheels strapped to it and she puts hamsters inside and makes them run as fast as possible. She's got a four-hamster-powered car. I don't know what she does if they're asleep.

Krazy Kow Saves The World – Well, Almost

What's the most important thing to learn in chemistry?
Don't lick the spoon.

A boy in our class thinks he's a light bulb.

Why don't you tell him he isn't?

What – and sit in the dark?

What amazing invention lets you see through walls? **Windows.**

Grumpfart went across to the synthesizer, fizzing and steaming with every step. The big machine was plugged in and powered up. A red light on top began to flash. 'The particle-synthe–' *SPPRRRGH!* – 'synthe–' *SPPRRRGH!* – 'synthe–' *SPPRRRGH!* – 'synthesizer is weady, mistwess.'

The old crone rummaged through the pile on her desk until she found a large saucepan that she connected to the wires on the synthesizer. This would keep the electrical charge circulating in the monster's body. She propped up the monster in her chair and rammed the pan down on the monster's head.

The Stitcher smiled. 'Hmmm. It's time for you to awake, my sweet!' she crooned, and flicked the switch.

Krankenstein's Crazy House of Horror

A skeleton is what's left after you've taken the insides out and the outside off.

Where does the chemistry teacher wash the dishes? **In the zinc.**

What's the difference between bird flu and swine flu? **If you catch bird flu, you need tweetment. If you get swine flu, you need oinkment.**

Our science teacher is very absent-minded. Last week he came into class with a box and said, 'In here I have a frog and a toad. We're going to find out the differences between them.' Then he opened the box, reached inside and took out two sandwiches. He looked at them and said, 'That explains why I didn't enjoy my lunch today.'

classroom chaos

Part Two

The Best Assembly EVER!

The next day Miss Pandemonium didn't even bother to use her siren on the way to school. She had far too much to do. She parked in the school playground and began to unload. Soon she had a tall pile of neatly folded boxes, which she carried into her classroom.

Shortly after that a strangely misshapen bunch of children began to arrive. Some carried cardboard boxes and some appeared to be struggling with jackets and coats that were alive. They wriggled and squiggled as if they were being tickled to bits. And as soon as they got into class they rushed to unzip themselves and, like magicians, they pulled out animals.

First there was a small dog. The dog was joined by another, bigger dog. The two dogs were soon joined by a lizard, a goat, three stick insects, a jar of frogspawn, five cats, eight rabbits, a snake (NOT poisonous!), two gerbils, nine hamsters, six guinea pigs, fifteen goldfish (in a tank), another three dogs, a few more cats, two budgerigars, a parrot, eight mice, three rats and a pony.

'He's called Tornado because he can run as fast as the wind,' Lily said proudly.

'He's lovely,' said Miss Pandemonium. 'Are you sure he needs so much straw? It seems to be getting everywhere.'

'That's in case he does a you-know-what,' Lily murmured confidentially.

'Oh. Well let's hope that he doesn't,' Miss Pandemonium whispered back.

Tyler was the last to arrive. He was holding something very carefully in his hands.

'What have you got there, Tyler?' Miss Pandemonium asked.

Tyler slowly opened his fingers and his new teacher peered into his cupped hands.

'Goodness, you've got quite a collection there. 'Ten woodlice, three worms and a couple of earwigs.'

'We don't have any pets. Mum says she's got me and doesn't need any more animals in the house,' said Tyler gruffly. 'So I found these on my way to school.'

'That was very clever of you, Tyler. You'd better pop outside and find some earth and stones and leaves for them.'

Miss Pandemonium settled her class to work. They were split into groups. One group worked on the boxes. A second group was put on painting duties. A third group was packed off to the library to do some research and the fourth group had the task of measuring things. Every half an hour or so Miss Pandemonium would swap the groups around so that nobody got bored and everyone did a bit of everything.

In the meantime one or two of the animals had managed to escape, so they kept the classroom door firmly shut, even though it might have been too late for that.

'They're bound to turn up sooner or later,' Miss Pandemonium said cheerfully. 'It's always the smallest ones that cause the most trouble, isn't it?'

Lily giggled. 'Mrs Snorkel is pretty small,' she pointed out.

Miss Pandemonium looked at her. 'I couldn't possibly comment,' she said, giving Lily a wink that was seen by almost everyone in class. They loved it, even Harry, who was still warning that dreadful things were going to happen.

'Miss Pandemonium is really going to catch it,' he declared. 'She's going to need a proper ambulance by the time Mrs Snorkel finishes with her. I think we ought to call it now.'

This worried some of the class. They knew that Harry was right. Nobody – NOBODY – was as dangerous as Mrs Snorkel when she was on the warpath.

By lunchtime Class Five were ready for their assembly. Miss Pandemonium went to the staffroom, flopped down in an armchair and opened her box of sandwiches.

'Oh dear,' she sighed. 'I seem to have put porridge

in my sandwiches.'

'You look worn out,' observed Mrs Waffitt. 'Have the children been giving you the runaround?'

'Not at all. They're charming,' Miss Pandemonium answered.

'Oh. It's just that you have wisps of straw in your hair.' Mrs Waffitt sniffed the air. 'There's a strange smell in here. It reminds me of – I'm not quite sure what. A zoo, I think, but that can't be right. There isn't an animal within a hundred metres of this school. Mrs Snorkel can't stand animals, you know. She's very sensitive.'

'What a shame. There seem to be quite a lot of things that Mrs Snorkel can't stand. Children, for example. I do find it strange that she should want to work in a school for children if she doesn't actually like them.'

Mrs Waffitt looked at Miss Pandemonium more closely. She leaned forward to whisper, 'I know. She is rather awful. We'd all like her to leave but, to be quite honest, we're scared. She's so terrifying. Um, I hope you don't mind me saying so, but there's a cheesy-bug crawling across your shoulder.'

'Cheesy-bug? Oh! A woodlouse. Is that what you call them? I wonder how it got there. I'll put it in my handbag.'

Miss Pandemonium opened her handbag and Mrs Waffitt got an even bigger shock. 'Oh my goodness, there's a mouse in your handbag.'

It was true. A little white mouse had just poked out his little pink nose, whiskers all a-quiver. Miss Pandemonium pushed the mouse back in and shut the bag.

'There. All gone.'

Mrs Waffitt had turned almost as white as the mouse. 'Don't let Mrs Snorkel see that. Please. PLEASE! Keep it out of her sight or there'll be such trouble.'

Miss Pandemonium patted Mrs Waffitt's shoulder comfortingly. 'Don't worry. I shall do my best. Well, I'm off. Lots to do. We're giving assembly this afternoon and I think you'll enjoy it. It's not to be missed.' Miss Pandemonium gave the other teacher a large wink. She was doing a lot of winking today.

* * *

The school hall filled with children as each class filed in for assembly and sat down. Soon everyone was there apart from Class Five.

Mrs Snorkel stood on a box at the front of the hall. She had to stand on a box otherwise not everyone could see her. Her arms were folded and her face was set in an intense scowl. She glanced at her watch and tut-tutted.

'Where is that wretched Class Five and their teacher?' she fumed. 'I thought they were giving assembly this afternoon?'

At that moment Miss Pandemonium herself strolled in. Mrs Snorkel watched and waited, searching for the children. 'Miss Pandemonium,' she snorted. 'You seem to have forgotten your class.'

'All in good time,' Miss Pandemonium said. 'Do go and sit down, Mrs Snorkel. Our assembly is about to start and I am sure you are going to enjoy our presentation.'

Miss Pandemonium went to the hall door and whispered to someone the other side. Maya came into the room, walked to the front and cleared her throat.

'Good afternoon, everyone. Today Class Five would like to present you with the story of Noah's Ark. Here to tell the story for you are Sunil and Harry.'

Now Sunil and Harry took centre stage and began to tell how Noah had built an ark and filled it with animals. Behind them Katie, Tyler and Marty were miming all the actions of building an ark and also providing all the sound effects.

'Then the storm began,' announced Harry.

'Spsssssh!' went Tyler very loudly.

'Bang, Crash!' went Katie and Marty, being the thunder.

'The water got higher and higher,' said Sunil. And Tyler acted out someone drowning.

'Glug gluggle glug! Aaargh! Glug! Save me! I can't swim!'

'All right, all right!' cried Mrs Snorkel. 'Do get on with it.'

'But Noah was safe on the ark with all the animals and it floated away across the sea,' chorused Harry and Sunil.

The double hall doors burst open and in came

the ark. It was huge and it was made of dozens of bits of cardboard. It just kept coming into the hall, more and more and more of it. This is what the children had been building and painting all morning. And it wasn't just the ark that came into the hall.

The animals came too. The ark had flaps cut into the sides and there they were, poking out their heads – REAL ANIMALS. There were dogs and cats and rabbits and parrots and a horse and a goat and a snake and mice and rats and hamsters and –

'AAAAARRRRRRGGGGGHHH!' screamed Mrs Snorkel. 'Get those creatures out of here! Aaaaarrrrrgggghhhh!' She leaped from her chair, sending it toppling backwards, and ran for the door. She tripped over poor Lily, went flying and crash-landed against the ark. The whole cardboard facade began to topple over and the animals panicked. Within seconds Mrs Snorkel had turned the assembly into a disaster zone. Creatures large and small were scurrying, jumping, slithering and galloping round the hall – and that included all the children – and the staff!

'The ark has sunk!' Tyler yelled, with considerable delight.

Everyone and everything went racing about the place, screaming, shouting and yelling. Doors were thrown open on to the playground and the chaos spread. Children and teachers and animals were all running around but nobody was quite sure whether the animals were chasing the people or if it was the other way round. As for Mrs Snorkel, she was last seen running and screaming from the school grounds, chased by a rather cute rabbit.

Class Five gradually rounded up their pets while the teachers rounded up their children and took them back to class. Nobody had been hurt and no animals injured. The only accident was when Tornado did a small you-know-what and Lily had to clear it up. In fact everyone – children AND teachers – thought it was the best assembly they had been to, EVER!

* * *

In the staffroom at the end of the day Miss Pandemonium made tea for herself and the other members of staff. 'What an exciting day,' she said.

Mrs Waffitt smiled. 'I have a feeling that when you go to a school it's probably nearly always an exciting day.'

The telephone rang. It was Mrs Snorkel.

'I have never, ever had such a terrible day at school. I am ringing to let you know that I am never, ever coming back. GOODBYE!!' The phone slammed down.

The cheer that went up from the staffroom almost blew the school roof off.

Teachers

How many teachers you have depends on how big your school is, really. Some primary schools only have one or two classes for everyone, from Reception to Year 6. Imagine that! If you don't get on with your teacher, you're really stuck. But some primary schools have more than twenty classes. Some secondary schools have more than fifty!

Teachers come in all shapes and sizes, and – this may come as a surprise – are almost all entirely human. They can get bored, and grumpy, and tired, and lonely, just like you. Some of them are mums and dads. You don't have to be their best friend. But it would really help to try to be nice to them.

Oh dear, did that bee sting you? We'd better put some cream on it.

Don't be stupid, miss — it'll be miles away by now.

Why can't you answer any of my questions?

Well, if I could, there wouldn't be much point in me being here.

Well, the good news is that your handwriting has got a lot better.

Thank you — but what's the bad news?

Now I can see how bad your spelling is.

I studied her carefully. I had always liked her. She seemed warm and cuddly, but there was also something unexpected about her. You never quite knew what she was going to say or do. I had a strong suspicion that not only did she dislike Mr Dedman, but that he knew she didn't like him. She had no time for people who threw their weight around, people like Gary Jarvis and the head.

Chicken School

Miss Comet was the youngest, prettiest and nicest teacher at Plumpot Primary School. Most of the other teachers were so old that they talked about the Age of the Dinosaurs as if they had been born then. In fact Dylan, who was nine, was pretty sure that some of the teachers really *were* dinosaurs. It was just that they hadn't quite fossilized yet, although they seemed well on the way.

Invasion of the Christmas Puddings

I wish you would pay just a little attention.

I'm paying as little attention as I can.

That's a very interesting outfit you're wearing, miss. Do you think it'll ever come back into fashion?

I take cleanliness very seriously at my school. Did you wipe your feet on the mat before you came into my office?

Oh, yes, sir.

I also insist pupils tell the truth. There is no mat outside my office.

I'm sorry, that's the wrong answer.

No, it isn't!

Look, let's meet halfway. I'll admit you're wrong, if you'll say I'm right.

Teacher Tracking

All of these teacher's names are hidden in the grid opposite. Use a pencil to draw a line through them all – they are in the order shown below. The line can go up, down or across but not diagonally. The line's been started for you, so off you go – and no cheating with all these teachers about!

PANDEMONIUM

EARWIGGER

SHRAPNELL

KUDDLE

DEDMAN

DOVE

RUMBLE

CROCK

DREW

P	A	N	N	E	L
N	O	D	P	A	L
I	M	E	H	R	K
U	E	R	S	D	U
M	G	G	I	D	L
E	A	R	W	D	E
E	V	O	D	E	D
R	U	M	N	A	M
E	L	B	K	D	R
C	R	O	C	W	E

Answers on page 137

Teacher assessment:
Miss Violet Pandemonium

Appearance: Unique. No one dresses like Miss Pandemonium. Or would want to. She sometimes smells rather unusual, and carries a large bag that appears to contain absolutely everything she owns (plants, books, food, clothes . . .).

Timekeeping: Variable. Miss Pandemonium is often available at short notice, which is admirable in a supply teacher, but she struggles to get to school on time. Incidentally, is she allowed to use the siren on that ambulance?

Respect for authority: Minimal. Miss Pandemonium manages to give the impression of agreeing with her superiors and doing what they ask, while her whole class sniggers and smirks because they know she is planning to disobey the instant their backs are turned.

Attitude: Overwhelmingly positive. She is alarmingly enthusiastic about everything she does, which makes the children eager and excited to learn. She is rather tiring, though, and there may be a large cleaning bill afterwards.

Recommendation: Approach with caution. Nothing may ever be the same at your school if you employ Miss Pandemonium.

Lesson Seven: Art & Music

There isn't a lesson that's art AND music. (Though it would be a lot of fun if there was.) But a lot of schools do art for one term and then music for the next. And they're subjects with things in common: they're fun, you don't get any homework, and the teachers are often ... unusual!

When you're little, parents seem quite proud of the art you bring home. However, after a couple of years of bringing home large sheets of coloured paper with splodges on, you'll notice that they don't seem quite so pleased.

Parents can also get enthusiastic about you learning a musical instrument. This can be hard, because it takes a lot of practice to get any good. So most children give up, using the clever tactic of 'Not Getting Any Better Despite Costing A Fortune'.

I like ballet, but I don't know why they spend so much time on tiptoe. Why don't they just get taller dancers?

I used to do tap dancing but I had to give up. I kept falling in the sink.

A waiter walked up to Vincent Van Gogh as he sat in a cafe and asked, 'Can I get you a cup of coffee?'
'No thanks,' replied Van Gogh. 'I've got one 'ere.'

Mrs Ruddlestone turned to the audience. 'Now we are going to hear a piece called *Ten Tin Soldiers*,' she announced. 'One, two, three . . .'

The march began. Ten pianos were playing beautifully together. Lucy held her breath. She was doing it! She glanced down at her fingers and began to panic. There were so many of them. How could she control all those wiggly fingers at the same time? Now nine pianos were playing together and one soldier had gone off course. His legs were crumpling and folding. Lucy looked at her music in despair. It was hopeless. She put her fingers down anywhere, everywhere, hoping to hit the right note.

Lightning Lucy Storms Ahead

Which composer was good at opening doors?
Handel.

Sign on the music room door:
**Gone out Chopin,
Bach in five minutes**

When does a singer stop being a singer?
When she becomes a little hoarse.

A boy in my class drew the teacher on the whiteboard.
He got into loads of trouble — it looked exactly like her.

What do musicians receive when they're sick?
Get-well-soon chords.

Lucy, if you don't stop playing that piano, I think I'll go crazy.

I think it's too late, Dad — I stopped playing an hour ago.

A rich man asked Picasso to paint his wife's portrait. When it was finished, the picture had three eyes and a nose on top of the head.

'That looks nothing like my wife,' the man complained.

'Why, what does she look like?' replied Picasso.

The man took a photo of his wife from his wallet and passed it over. Picasso stared at it.

'She's very small, isn't she?' he said.

Our school orchestra is very badly behaved.
They don't know how to conduct themselves.

I've got an elastic trumpet. **I play in a rubber band.**

Which big opera singer wore a Burberry cap? **Chavarotti.**

How do you mend a broken trumpet? **With a tuba glue.**

I hate Country Dancing. Miss Pettigrew goes to an Irish dancing club and she makes us do it as well. We have to stand there with our arms quite still and make our legs flip about all over the place. Sanjeev always manages to fall over and knock down everyone else. We end up looking like some sort of World Champion Pick-Up-Sticks Competition. I think he does it deliberately.

The Beak Speaks

What do you think of my piano playing?

I think you should be on the telly.

Really? You think I'm that good?

No, you're rubbish. But if you were on the telly, I could turn you off.

Miss Earwigger stormed into Miss Pandemonium's class, where the teacher was thumping away at a piano while the whole class were singing at the tops of their voices and banging on their desks.

'Miss Pandemonium!' screeched Miss Earwigger. 'Do you know my class can't concentrate for all this terrible racket?'

'No,' said Miss Pandemonium. 'But you hum it, and I'll try to play along.'

'Paul, give a sheet of this paper to everyone. Now, who can tell me what origami is?'

'Is she a pop star, miss?' asked Kerry.

'That's brilliant! What a wonderful name! Actually, *origami* is a Japanese word and it means the art of folding paper. Paul's just given you a sheet of origami paper and I want you to fold it into a triangle, like this.'

Everyone busily folded their sheet. The door whizzed open. 'Maths?' enquired Mr Shrapnell, glaring suspiciously.

'Hold up your shapes, Class Three,' cried Miss Pandemonium. 'What are they?'

'Triangles!' shouted the class.

Mr Shrapnell frowned, growled, shut the door and went away. The children looked at each other and grinned. This was great.

Pandemonium at School

What do you call an American drawing?
A Yankee doodle.

Spot it or Not

Artists need a good eye for detail. Can you spot six differences between these two pictures?

Answers on page 137

Pupil Assessment: Lucy King

Music: Lucy has been playing piano for some time now. Mrs Ruddlestone says she can be quite good, but she struggles to concentrate. When she makes mistakes, she quickly gets frustrated, which only makes things worse. Her performances have often been interrupted by strange events.

Sport: Lucy has been a real asset to the school football team, playing a significant part in our recent success. In ways I don't understand we just seem to be much luckier when she's around.

Geography: Lucy has improved a lot this term. She drew a remarkable map recently: a birds-eye view that looked like she'd actually flown over the town.

Form teacher's notes: This term has seen some remarkable events in class, including a fire and some episodes of floating. Lucy has shown she performs very well in a crisis, saving pupils or protecting the school from further damage on several occasions. However, she got quite stressed by these events, almost as if they were her fault.

Lesson Eight: Sport

The one thing that drives sports teachers totally bonkers is someone who is really good at sport, but doesn't want to do it competitively. They just don't understand that you may not want to practise hard, beat people, win prizes and show off. Your English teacher doesn't insist you take part in a poetry competition every single Saturday. Maths teachers don't make you do extra sums every evening because you're good at them. What is it with sports teachers? Why can't we just do sports and games because we enjoy them?

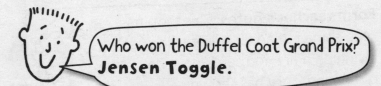

Who won the Duffel Coat Grand Prix? **Jensen Toggle.**

OK, class – time for your exercises. Up, down, up down, up down, up, down . . . and relax. Right, now the other eyelid.

Why can't cars play football?
They've only got one boot each.

I would have been player of the match if it wasn't for two things. **The referee and the rules.**

What do elephants like to play on a car journey?
Squash.

What's the chilliest football ground in the Premier League?
Cold Trafford.

Stop, don't dive in the pool – there's no water in it!

That's OK, I can't swim.

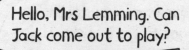

Hello, Mrs Lemming. Can Jack come out to play?

Oh no, it's far too cold.

OK. Can his football come out to play, then?

Belinda looked slowly about the palace hall. Standing at the foot of the stairs was a large stone statue of a previous king. Belinda walked silently up to it, gazed at it for a few moments, then suddenly,

'Aaaaa-HA!' She gave a great yell, spun round on one foot at the centre of the statue. There was a splinter of breaking stone and the statue cracked into two separate halves. Even as the top section toppled to the floor, Belinda raised her right arm and sliced the head off with a single blow of her bare hand. Stormbelly screamed. 'Stop! That's your great-grandfather!'

The Karate Princess

One kid in our team was told he needed to get fitter, and should go for a five-kilometre run every night. **Last time we heard, he'd got to Moscow.**

Do you know why we call our goalie Cinderella? **Because he keeps running away from the ball.**

Why does your school have a triangular football pitch?

Someone took a corner.

I'm sorry I missed that penalty, captain. I don't know what went wrong, it was such an easy shot. I'm so annoyed, I could kick myself!

I wouldn't bother. You'd probably miss.

I had to stop playing rugby when I broke a toe.
It was someone else's.

A javelin thrower called Vicky
Found the grip of her javelin sticky.
When it came to the throw,
She couldn't let go –
Making judging the distance quite tricky.

I've just run 100 metres in six seconds!

**Wow, that's incredible —
that's a new world record!**

Ah, it won't count. I cheated –
I took a short cut.

You have a referee in football, and an umpire in cricket, but what do you have in bowls?
Cornflakes.

I had the ball at my feet and the goal was right in front and everyone was shouting and yelling, and my foot smashed into the ball. Away it soared and the goalkeeper jumped and his arms went up and the ball whizzed straight over his hands and into the net. Brilliantissimo! I had scored! Me! Jack! Scored!

I turned and ran back down the pitch and I did The Slide. You know, when you score and you throw yourself down on your knees and you slide across the grass. Wonderful!

Unless it's AstroTurf. If it's AstroTurf it isn't like sliding on grass. It's like sliding across a cheese grater. I took all the skin off my knees. Talk about OW!

Beware! Killer Tomatoes

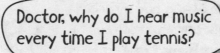
Doctor, why do I hear music every time I play tennis?

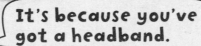
It's because you've got a headband.

Why was Cinderella rubbish at football?
Because her coach was a pumpkin.

Did you hear about what happened when the Karate Princess joined the army?
The first time she saluted, she knocked herself out.

I was standing in the middle of a field, idly wondering why the football was getting bigger and bigger.
Then it hit me.

Two balls of string had a race. Which one won?
Neither, they tied.

I took Nicholas to a football match, but when we got there I couldn't find the tickets. 'Run home and see if I left them there, Nicholas,' I asked.

Half an hour later Nicholas came back, just as the game was about to start.

'Yes, Dad – you left them at home,' he said. 'The tickets are on the kitchen table.'

They peered into the hall, but Mrs Earwigger was in there talking a PE lesson with Class Six. The children watched in fascination as eleven totally silent children climbed up ropes, balanced on benches and did forward rolls on the mats.

'How does she get them so quiet?' whispered Cleo. 'It's not natural.'

'And what's happened to the rest of the class?' asked Mike.

Samantha simply pointed to the far end of the hall. A long line of twenty-one children stood silently facing the wall, with their hands on their heads.

Pirate Pandemonium

Monster Match

Which of these shadows is the right one to match this picture of Jodie?

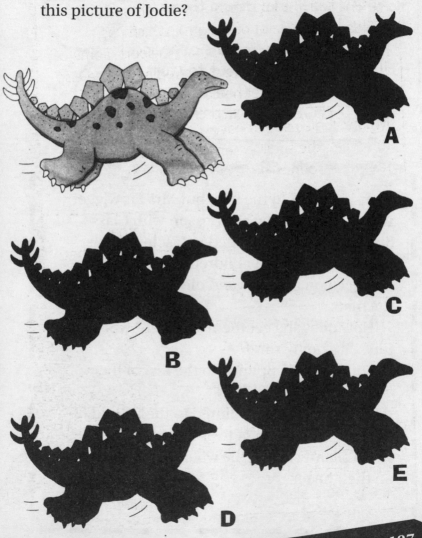

Answers on page 137

Pupil Assessment:
Jodie Bolton

Sport: Jodie has put on some weight recently (actually, quite a lot of weight), which has affected her ability to take part in sport. Some of the equipment will have to be replaced. She also needs a much bigger netball skirt.

Music: Jodie used to have a pleasant voice, but this week she spoilt assembly with her attempts to sing. It sounds like a croaky roar. Might some throat sweets help?

Science: Jodie has recently become rather dismissive of science, claiming, for instance, that doctors talk a lot of rubbish. I have no idea what caused this change of attitude.

Form teacher's notes: Jodie has been rather isolated at school, with some of the girls making cruel jokes about her appearance. She is more than capable of fighting back, however. Incidentally, she needs to bring in her own lunch; we can't afford to lose any more plants.

And Finally: The Holidays

When you're one week into the autumn term, the summer holidays may seem a really long time ago and the Christmas break feels like it will never come. But remember you spend an impressive 175 days every year NOT at school. And if you're really lucky, you'll get to go away for some of those 175 days. Probably not that many, though. Your parents don't get nearly as much holiday time as you. (Unless they're teachers.)

I wanted to buy Mum some lipstick for Christmas, but I didn't know what size her mouth was.

Will the Christmas pudding be long, Mum?

No, it'll be round like last year.

What do reindeer hang on their Christmas trees? Horn-aments.

That train set is fantastic, I'll take it.

Certainly, sir. A very good choice — I'm sure your son will love it.

Would he? You're probably right. I'd better get two, then.

Doctor, I keep stealing things when I go out Christmas shopping. Can you give me anything to make me stop?

Well, these pills should help. If they haven't worked in a week, can you get me an iPhone?

This unbreakable toy car you sold me for my son is terrible, I want my money back.

Why? Don't tell me it's broken!

Oh, no. But he used it to break every other toy he owns.

Dad, I don't want to go on holiday to Australia any more.

Shut up and keep swimming!

'Why is there only one day for Christmas? It's so much work. I've got parcels coming out of my ears. Other people get the whole year to do things. I get one day. And that's a holiday for everyone, except me. It's not fair.'

'There, there, calm down, my big red jellybean. At least you have your lovely new sleigh.'

Invasion of the Christmas Puddings

FC1

We went on holiday to a place so dull, one day the tide went out and never came back.

We went on holiday with a very cheap airline. First the stewardess told us to fasten our Sellotape. And the plane only had an outside toilet.

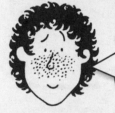

That's nothing. Our plane was so cheap, we had to open the windows, put out an arm and flap.

The in-flight movie was rubbish. But I don't think that man should have walked out.

It was so hot on our holiday, we had to take it in turns to sit in each other's shadow.

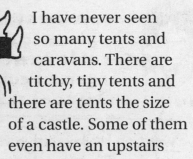

I have never seen so many tents and caravans. There are titchy, tiny tents and there are tents the size of a castle. Some of them even have an upstairs bit. No, just kidding! But they are definitely enormous, and all colours – red, green, brown ones and blue ones. Some people even have stripy tents and one tent has a skull and crossbones flag flying outside. They must be pirates on holiday.

My Brother's Famous Bottom Goes Camping

We left our house in a bit of a mess when we went on holiday. In fact, while we were away, burglars broke in and tidied up.

Our hotel room was so small, when Dad put the key in the lock he broke the window. And the walls were so thin, I could hear the people next door thinking.

I'd like to complain about the roof on our holiday apartment.

Why, what about it?

We'd like one.

So, thanks to Lucy, the whole family went off to Greece for four weeks.

They had a wonderful time. They swam and sunbathed and saw all the sights. They danced themselves silly at the discos and ate strange food. Nicholas found a baby octopus when he went diving and wanted to bring it home, but Mum wouldn't let him. The only time Lucy had to use her special power was when Nicholas fell over the balcony rail. She whizzed down in a shower of sparks and grabbed him before he hit the ground. She was getting used to that sort of thing.

Lightning Lucy Strikes Again

EXAM TIME!

Right, settle down and face the front! It's time to find out how much attention you've been paying to all those silly Jeremy Strong books. You have twenty minutes to answer these questions. No peeking at your neighbour's answers, or I'll send you to the head teacher.

1 At which school is Mr Dedman the head teacher ?

....

2 Who is the youngest, prettiest and nicest teacher at Plumpot Primary School?

....

3 What does Miss Pettigrew like to do in her spare time?

....

....

4 Who does Mr Shrapnell, head teacher at Dullandon Primary, get as a replacement when one of his teachers is sick?

. . . .

5 Who does Siggy the Viking call Crumble?

. . . .

6 Jamie Frink (creator of Krazy Kow) has an eco-mad head teacher. What's her name?

. . . .

7 In *I'm Telling You, They're ALIENS!*, what instrument does Rob Smith play?

. . . .

8 What does Miss Pandemonium let Class Five at Witts End Primary pretend to be during Book Week?

. . . .

9 Who is Jodie Bolton's teacher?

. . . .

10 Who is Lightning Lucy's piano teacher?

. . . .

And Finally...

Grown-ups like to say that your schooldays are the best time of your life. This is because they've forgotten all the boring and not-fun bits.

The good bits are pretty good, though. You make friends you may keep for the rest of your life; you get long holidays; and you don't have too many responsibilities. You may even go to school with a future celebrity – or a dinosaur.

So make the most of school (and – on behalf of your teachers – don't cause too much chaos).

ANSWERS

Education confusion p. 12

The lessons are Art; English; History; Maths; Geography; Science; Sport; Music.

Creature count p. 27

Thirteen chickens, one cockerel, two goats, two tortoises, two cats and a crocodile – making 21 animals in total.

Sennapod Shadows p. 35

A – 5; B – 3; C – 2; D – 1; E – 4.

Connect Two p. 57

Software; Database; Keyboard; Broadband; Laptop; Joystick; Mainframe; Password; Website; Download; Online.

Lunch Lines p. 66

Line B leads to the plate of food.

Cracking Crossword p. 76

```
                              N
        H           W       T H O R
    D E N M A R K             S
  H   D           E           E
  O   E   F       S           P
  T I B B L E T H W A I T E
  E   Y   O       L           C       L
  L       T       I           K       L
          B       N           E       I
          Y       G       H O R N S
```